شرح
القواعد الأربعة

An Explanation of Muḥammad Ibn ʿAbdul-Wahhāb's Four Principles of *Shirk*

Translation and Commentary by

Abu Ammaar Yasir Qadhi

ISBN 1 898649 52 9

British Library Cataloguing in Publication Data.

A catalogue record for this book is available from the British Library.

Published: Al-Hidaayah Publishing and Distribution

Distributed by: Al-Hidaayah Publishing and Distribution
P.O. Box 3332
Birmingham
United Kingdom
B10 0UH

Tel: 0121 753 1889
Fax: 0121 753 2422
Website: www.al-hidaayah.co.uk
Email: mail@al-hidaayah.co.uk

Printed by Interprint Limited, Malta

شَرْحُ
القَوَاعِدِ الأَرْبَعَةِ

An Explanation of
Muḥammad Ibn ʿAbdul-Wahhāb's
Four Principles of *Shirk*

Contents

Transliteration Table ... 7

Foreword ... 9

A Short Biography of Muḥammad ibn ʿAbd al-Wahhāb ... 13

The Arabic Text ... 18

The English Translation of the Text ... 23

- The First Principle ... 24
- The Second Principle ... 24
- The Third Principle ... 25
- The Fourth Principle ... 27

The Explanation of *The Four Principles of Shirk* ... 29

Introduction ... 30

- Worship: Goals and Definition ... 33
- *Tawḥīd* and *Shirk* ... 37
- Importance of Knowing *Shirk* ... 38

The First Principle ... 41

The Second Principle ... 44

- The *Jāhilīyyah* Arabs Understood the Concept of *ʿIbādah* ... 47
- The Concept of Intercession ... 48

The Third Principle ... 51

The Fourth Principle ... 55

- Calling a Muslim a Disbeliever ... 58

Conclusion ... 60

Transliteration Table

Consonants,

ء	'	د	d	ض	ḍ	ك	k
ب	b	ذ	dh	ط	ṭ	ل	l
ت	t	ر	r	ظ	ẓ	م	m
ث	th	ز	z	ع	ʿ	ن	n
ج	j	س	s	غ	gh	ه	h
ح	ḥ	ش	sh	ف	f	و	w
خ	kh	ص	ṣ	ق	q	ي	y

Vowels, diphthongs, etc.

Short:	ـَ	a	ـِ	i	ـُ	u
Long:	ـَا	ā	ـِي	ī	ـُو	ū
diphthongs:			ـَيْ	ay	ـَوْ	aw

Foreword

All Praise is due to Allāh, who created us to worship Him, for He said:

وَمَا خَلَقْتُ الْجِنَّ وَالْإِنسَ إِلَّا لِيَعْبُدُونِ ﴿٥٦﴾

And I did not create men or *jinn* except to worship Me.[1]

And may peace and blessings be upon the Prophet Muḥammad ibn ʿAbdillāh, the greatest of all men, and the most noble of all prophets, who came with the simple message of Islām, the essence of which is to worship Allāh alone.

قُلْ هَٰذِهِۦ
سَبِيلِيٓ أَدْعُوٓا۟ إِلَى ٱللَّهِ ۚ عَلَىٰ بَصِيرَةٍ أَنَا۠ وَمَنِ ٱتَّبَعَنِى ۖ وَسُبْحَٰنَ
ٱللَّهِ وَمَآ أَنَا۠ مِنَ ٱلْمُشْرِكِينَ ﴿١٠٨﴾

Say (O Muḥammad): This is my path, I call to Allāh, upon clear knowledge. I (do this) and those that follow me, and Allāh is Exalted and Glorified (over all imperfections that others attribute to Him). And I am not of those who commit *shirk*.[2]

From this verse, it is seen that the call of the Prophet (ﷺ) – in fact, the call of all the prophets – is to Allāh. This call comprises of two aspects: the knowledge and recognition of who Allāh is (and this is known in Arabic as *tawḥīd al-ʿitiqādī*), and the singling out of Allāh in worship, so that none is worshipped except Allāh (and this is known as *tawḥīd al-ʿamalī*).

So the first matter involves purifying one's conception of Allāh, and ascribing to Him the Most Perfect Names and Noble Attributes. It involves negating the existence of any object or deity that has the capability of creating, sustaining, nourishing or controlling the creation except for Allāh. It involves affirming the Perfect existence of Allāh, having no partners or sons.

And the second matter involves purifying one's actions of worship, so that none except Allāh is worshipped. This is a logical consequence of the first aspect of

---

[1] Sūrah *al-Dhāriyāt*, verse 56.

[2] Sūrah *Yūsuf*, verse 108.

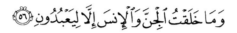

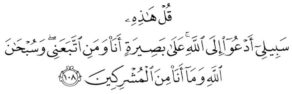

tawḥīd, for if one affirms that only Allāh is the Creator and Sustainer, and has complete Power and Control over the creation, then it follows that only Allāh deserves to be worshipped. Even though this might appear to be a simple fact for many, unfortunately most of mankind has deviated from this simple principle. This is because they affirm the Existence of Allāh, and that He is the ultimate Creator and Sustainer. However, for various reasons, they direct their acts of worship to other than Allāh.

And this is a matter that is in direct opposition to the noble goal and dignified purpose for which mankind was created, for it is *shirk* (associating of partners along with Allāh).

Before the advent of the Prophet (ﷺ), *shirk* was rampant all over the world, including the land of Arabia, where the Prophet (ﷺ) himself was sent. By the Will of Allāh, the Prophet (ﷺ) and early Muslims were able to eliminate *shirk* in all of its forms from the entire peninsula of Arabia, and eventually many surrounding areas as well. However, with the passage of time, innovations crept into the Muslim nation, and these innovations eventually led to acts of *shirk*. So it was, that hardly a thousand years after the Prophet's (ﷺ) death, open acts of *shirk* were being committed in the very peninsula where the Prophet (ﷺ) preached.

Strangely though, these acts were not being committed by people alien to Islām, or by idol-worshippers who professed enmity to Allāh and His Messenger. Rather, they were being committed by people who claimed to be Muslims, and, even worse, were trying to justify their *shirk* from the Qur'ān and sunnah. People were openly calling out to graves and saints, asking such 'holy' people to grant them their desires, and to save them from their distress. Large monuments were built over the graves of such saints, and people travelled long distances to worship at these sites. In other areas, blessings were sought from trees and rocks, and people would seek help from other than Allāh. To add to all this, sorcery and fortune-telling were rampant amongst the masses, and both of these acts are manifestations of *shirk*.

Such was the situation in which Allāh sent a reviver, a *mujāddid*,[3] who called the people once again to the pristine Islām and the pure monotheism that the

---

[3] A *mujāddid* is one who guides the people back to Islām after they have deviated from it. So he calls them to return to the beliefs of the Prophet (ﷺ) and Companions, and warns them against innovations. From this, we understand the mistake of those who claim that a *mujāddid* is one who innovates a new philosophy and understanding of Islām. The Prophet (ﷺ) said,

> "Indeed, Allāh the Exalted sends, after every one hundred years, someone who renovates (*yujaddid*) for them their religion."

Reported by Abū Dawūd; (see *al-Ṣaḥīḥah*, # 599).

Prophet (ﷺ) came with. He warned them of the blatant *shirk* that they were doing, and exhorted them to return to the Qur'ān and sunnah to understand their religion. This man was Muḥammad ibn 'Abd al-Wahhāb.

Although a lot of confusion and false propaganda exists about this personality, perhaps the easiest way to clarify this *Imām's* message is to read his works. In his works, the Muslim finds that the author hardly speaks himself; rather, he lets the Qur'ān and sunnah do the talking for him. The reader finds refreshingly simple sentences and phrases, full of beneficial knowledge, and overflowing with benefit. And every single point that the Shaykh brings forth is backed up with an *āyah* of the Qur'ān, or a ḥadith of the Prophet (ﷺ).

So when one studies this Shaykh's works, far from finding them to be full of deviated concepts and alien philosophies, he finds them to be calling to the pure, pristine Islām, free of superstitious beliefs and ignorant customs. In fact, one of the trademarks of the works of this *Imām* is that he hardly ever quotes anything besides the Qur'ān and sunnah. It is due to this reason that his works are studied all over the world, at all different levels; for a child can read them, and gain some benefit, and a scholar can read them, and be able to extract many points of benefit.

Although the works of this great scholar are many, some of them are more famous than others. However, not much attention has been given to his works in the English language, and therefore the need was felt to translate his more important works, not just so that the English audience benefit from his knowledge, but also to expel the false propaganda that surrounds his persona. By reading his works directly, the reader can judge for himself what the Shaykh called to, instead of basing such judgements on the lies of his enemies.

A short biography of Muḥammad ibn 'Abd al-Wahhāb follows this foreword, in which the primary works of his are listed. The work that is in the reader's hand is one of the shortest works that he wrote, entitled *al-Qawā'id al-Arba'ah*, or *The Four Principles.* (Since these principles deal with *shirk*, the English title of the book was modified to *The Four Principles of Shirk*).

Although the actual tract itself is extremely short – perhaps only four pages in the original Arabic – it is full of benefit, and lays down clear principles that are essential in order to understand the essence of *shirk*. It is no exaggeration to state that, without understanding these simple principles, one does not have a complete and clear picture of the actuality of this grave sin.

I was very fortunate and blessed to be able to attend an explanation of this short treatise by one of the leading scholars of our times, the *'Allāmah*, *Imām* 'Abdullāh ibn Jibrīn, may Allāh protect him, and found it extremely beneficial. It was while attending this *sharḥ* (explanation) that I first conceived the idea to translate this simple work, and Shaykh Ibn Jibrīn's *sharḥ* also formed the basis of my own explanation. I also relied upon some of the material that we studied in the Master's level courses that I took in the Department of *'Aqīdah* at the University of Madīnah, and upon the explanation of the *Qawā'id* by Shaykh Sāliḥ Āl al-Shaykh (who is one of the descendants of the author).

The actual translation of the text of *Qawā'id al-Arba'ah*, without any explanation, is produced immediately after this introduction, followed by a point-by-point explanation of each principle. The reader is requested to read the entire tract first at least two or three times, so that he or she understands the general theme of the book, and then move on to the explanation of the text. In this manner, the reader will have a complete picture of the four principles, and will be able to benefit from the explanation in a fuller manner.

The work in the reader's hands is complementary to another work of the Shaykh, entitled *Kashf al-Shubuhāt*, which I am presently translating as well, along with an explanatory text. In this second piece of work, which is more advanced than this one, I elaborate on the origins of *shirk*, the types of *shirk*, the reasons that people commit *shirk*, and the evidences that ignorant Muslims who worship other than Allāh try to use to justify their *shirk*, along with a refutation of those evidences. The reader is therefore requested to benefit from both works in order to gain a more complete knowledge and understanding of *shirk*.

I would like to thank Naseem Khan, who helped in the initial draft of the translation of this work, and 'Abd al-Qayūm, 'Abd al-Awwal and Ahsan who helped in proof-reading the text.

May Allāh guide us to the Straight Path – the Path of those whom He has favoured with *tawḥīd*, and saved from *shirk*.

Abu Ammaar Yasir Qadhi
Al-Madīnah al-Nabawiyyah – The City of the Prophet (ﷺ)
5th Dhul Qa'dah, 1421 A.H. ; 30th January, 2001 C.E.

A Short Biography of Muḥammad ibn ʿAbd al-Wahhāb

He is Abū al-Ḥusayn Muḥammad ibn ʿAbd al-Wahhāb ibn Sulaymān ibn Alī ibn Musharrif al-Wuhaybī, from the tribe of Tamīm.[4] He was born in the city of ʿUyaynah, which is in the middle of the Arabian Peninsula, in the year 1115 A.H. (1704 C.E.). He was from a family of scholars and learned men, for his father, ʿAbd al-Wahhāb ibn Sulaymān (d. 1153 A.H.) was one of the famous scholars of Najd, and the *Qāḍī* (religious judge) of ʿUyaynah. And his grandfather, Sulaymān ibn Alī (d. 1079 A.H.) was also well-known for his knowledge, as was his uncle Ibrāhīm ibn Sulaymān.

He memorised the Qur'ān before he was ten years old, and learnt from many scholars in his area, including his father and uncle. He also travelled to Madīnah and Iraq to study with its scholars. In Madīnah, he met and studied with the famous Indian scholar Muḥammad Ḥayat al-Sindī (d. 1165 A.H.), and was greatly impressed with him, as was the teacher with his student. He also studied with the ḥadīth scholar ʿAbdullāh ibn Sālim al-Baṣrī (d. 1134 A.H.), and the famous scholar ʿAbdullāh ibn Sayf.

As for his students, they are too many to be numbered. Foremost amongst them were his sons, Ḥusayn, ʿAlī, ʿAbdullāh and Ibrāhīm, and his grandson ʿAbd al-Rahmān ibn Ḥasan, who authored the famous *Fatḥ al-Majīd Sharḥ Kitāb al-Tawḥīd*. Also amongst his students are: ʿAbd al-ʿAzīz ibn Muḥammad ibn Saʿūd (d. 1218 A.H.), Ḥamad ibn Nāṣir ibn Mu'ammar (d. 1225 A.H.), and ʿAbd al-ʿAzīz ibn ʿAbdullāh ibn Ḥussayin (d. 1237 A.H.).

He wrote many works, in ḥadīth, *tafsīr*, *fiqh*, and general topics. However, his primary focus was *ʿaqīdah*. The following is a list of his more famous works:

1- *Kitāb al-Tawḥīd.* This book without a doubt is the spearhead of the Shaykh's *daʿwah,* and his most famous work.[5]

---

[4] Most of this biography is taken from the introduction to *Fatḥ al-Majīd*, pps. 14-20.

[5] Although the work has been translated a number of times, none of these translations explains the work in a detailed manner. Perhaps one of the more useful translations is the one by Sameh Strauch (International Islamic Publishing House, Riyadh, 1998 A.H.), entitled *The Book of Tawhīd*.

2- *Usūl al-Thalāthah.* A basic introductory level text concerning the fundamentals of Islām.[6]

3- *al-Qawā'id al-Arba'ah.* The present work, dealing with the fundamentals of *shirk*.

4- *Kashf al-Shubuhāt.* A refutation of the most common arguments that are used by those who commit *shirk* to justify their actions.[7]

5- *Mukhtaṣar al-Sīrah.*

6- *Mukhtaṣar Fatḥ al-Bārī.*

7- *Mukhtaṣar Zād al-Ma'ād.*

8- *Masā'il al-Jāhiliyyah.*

9- *Adab al-Mashy ilā al-Ṣalāt.*

10- *Tafsīr Sūrat al-Ikhlās.*

And many other works. Most of his works were compiled and printed under the title *Majmū'ah Mu'alafāt al-Shaykh Muḥammad ibn 'Abd al-Wahhāb*.[8]

He wrote in one of his letters, when he was asked what he calls to, "And I am not, *alḥamdulillāh*, one of those who calls to the belief of the *Sūfis*,[9] or (the blind

---

[6] The explanation of *Usūl al-Thalāthah* by Shaykh Muḥammad ibn Sālih al-'Uthaymīn was translated by Br. Dawūd Burbank entitled "Explanation of the Three Fundamental Principles of Islaam", and published by Al-Hidaayah Publishing & Distribution (Birmingham, 1998). Another translation is also being prepared.

[7] This work, along with a commentary, is presently being translated by the author.

[8] Printed in Riyadh, 1398 A.H., under the supervision of *Imām* Muḥammad ibn Sa'ūd Islamic University.

[9] The term *Sūfi* is applied to a spectrum of different groups and cults, all of which differ slightly with each other. Therefore, it is difficult to give a precise definition that encompasses all of these groups. However, these groups have a number of commonalities, including: 1– extreme exaggeration of saints and 'holy' people, both dead and alive (which in many cases leads to blatant *shirk*); 2 – a perverted concept of piety, which involves leaving many matters that are permitted in Islām, and instead worshipping Allāh through innovated methods; 3 – an indifference to the knowledge of the Qur'ān and sunnah, and an apathy to studious learning of the sciences of the religion (this is based on their belief that every single verse in the Qur'ān has an 'outer' and 'inner' meaning, and the 'inner' meaning is gained, not through religious knowledge, but through asceticism and acts of worship).

following) of a *faqīh*,[10] or one of the philosophical groups,[11] or even to one of the scholars that I myself respect, such as Ibn al-Qayyim, al-Dhahabī, Ibn Kathīr, and others. Rather, I call to Allāh alone, for He is One, having no partners, and I call to the sunnah of the Prophet (ﷺ). And this is what he (ﷺ) commanded the first of his nation, and the last of them. And I hope that I will not reject any truth if it comes to me. Rather, I call Allāh, and His angels, and the entire creation to witness, that if a word comes from you that is true, then of a surety I will accept it with all respect, and I will throw against the wall everything that goes against it, from the statements of all the scholars that I respect, except for the Prophet (ﷺ), for he is the only one that speaks nothing but the truth."[12]

In another letter, in response to a query posed to him by one of the scholars of Iraq, he wrote, "I wish to inform you that I am – by the blessings of Almighty Allāh – a follower (of the scholars of the past), and not an innovator. My beliefs and my religion that I consider to be correct in the sight of Allāh is the belief of *Ahl al-Sunnah wal-Jamā' ah*, and this is what the scholars of the Muslims are upon, such as the four great *Imāms* (i.e., Abū Ḥanīfah, Mālik, al-Shāfi'ī, and Aḥmad ibn Ḥanbal), and those that truly follow them until the Day of Judgement. However, (all I have done is that) I have explained to the people the importance of sincerity in worshipping Allāh, and I have warned them against making *du' ā* to the living or dead of the saints and others besides them. I have warned them against associating partners with Allāh and directing acts of worship that are specific for Allāh (to others). (Examples of such acts are) sacrificing, and vowing, and *tawakkul* (depending upon someone), and prostrating, and other acts that are rights only due to Allāh. No one deserves to be associated along with Allāh in these acts, neither a close angel, nor a prophet. And this message is what all the prophets called to, from the first of them to the last of them, and this is what the *Ahl al-Sunnah wal-Jamā' ah* are upon."[13]

He died in the year 1206 A.H. (1792 C.E.), at the ripe age of 91. Many of the famous scholars praised him highly, such as al-Sana'ānī (d. 1182 A.H.), and al-Shawkanī (d. 1255 A.H.). May Allāh reward the Shaykh, and grant him the highest of Paradise!

---

[10] A scholar of jurisprudence. He is pointing out that he is not of those that call to the obligation of blindly following a particular religious scholar, or *madh-hab*.

[11] Referring to those Islamic sects that were based on or influenced by Greek philosophy, such as the *Mu'tazilah*, the *Ash' arīs*, and the *Māturidis*.

[12] *Majmū' Mu'alafāt*, (5/252).

[13] *Majmū' Mu'alafāt*, (5/36).

The Text of
The Four Principles of *Shirk*

The Arabic Text

القواعد الأربع

لشيخ الإسلام الإمام المجدد
الشيخ محمد بن عبد الوهاب

ـــ رحمه الله ـــ

بسم الله الرحمن الرحيم

أسأَلُ اللهَ الكَرِيم رَبَّ العَرْشِ العَظِيمِ أن يَتَوَلاَّكَ في الدُّنيا وَالآخِرَة، وَأن يَجْعَلَكَ مُبارَكـــاً أيْنَمَا كُنْتَ، وَأن يَجْعَلَكَ مِمّن إذا أُعْطِيَ شَكَرَ، وَإذَا ابْتُلِيَ صَبَرَ، وَإذَا أذْنَبَ اسْتَغْفَر، فَإنَّ هَذِهِ الثَّلاثَ عُنْوَانُ السَّعَادَة.

اعْلَمْ ـــ أرْشَدَكَ اللهُ لِطَاعَتِهِ ـــ : أنَّ الْحَنِيفِيَّةَ مِلَّةَ إبْراهِيم : أنْ تَعْبُدَ اللهَ وَحْدَهُ مُخْلِصـــاً لَهُ الدِّيْن كَمَا قَالَ ـــ تَعالَى ـــ

﴿ وَمَا خَلَقْتُ الْجِنَّ وَالإنْسَ إلاّ لِيَعْبُدُون ﴾ سورة الذاريات [٥٦-٥١]

فَإذَا عَرَفْتَ أنَّ اللهَ خَلَقَكَ لِعِبادَتِهِ فَاعْلَمْ : أنَّ الْعِبادَةَ لاَ تُسَمَّى عِبَادَةً إلاّ مَعَ التَّوْحِيد، كَمَا أنَّ الصَّلاةَ لا تُسَمَّى صَلاَةً إلاّ مَعَ الطَّهارَة، فَإذَا دَخَلَ الشِّرْكُ في العِبَادَةِ فَسَدَتْ كَالحَدَثِ إذا دَخَلَ فِي الطَّهارَة.

فَإذا عَرَفْتَ أنَّ الشِّركَ إذا خَالَطَ العِبَادَةَ أفسَدَها وَأحبَطَ العَمَلَ وَصارَ صَاحِبُهُ مِنَ الْخَالِدِيْنَ فِي النَّار عَرَفْتَ أنَّ أهَمَّ مَا عَلَيكَ : مَعْرِفَةُ ذَلِكَ، لَعَلَّ اللهَ أنْ يُخَلِّصَكَ مِنْ هَذِه الشَّبَكَةِ، وَهِيَ الشِّرْكُ باللهِ الَّذِي قَالَ اللهُ تَعَالَى فِيه:

﴿ إِنَّ اللهَ لا يَغْفِرُ أَنْ يُشْرَكَ بِهِ وَيَغْفِرُ مَا دُوْنَ ذَلِكَ لِمَنْ يَشَاء ﴾ سورة النساء [٤-١١٦]

وَذَلِكَ بمَعْرِفَةِ أَرْبَعَةِ قَوَاعِدَ ذَكَرَهَا اللهُ ـــ تَعَالَى ـــ فِي كِتَابه

القَاعِدَةُ الأولَى

أنْ تَعْلَمَ أنَّ الْكُفَّارَ الَّذِينَ قَاتَلَهُمْ رَسُولُ اللهِ صَلَّى اللهُ عَلَيْهِ وَسَلَّمَ يُقِرّونَ بأنَّ اللهَ ـــ تَعَالَى ـــ هُوَ الْخَالِقُ الرَّازِقُ الْمُدَبِّر، وَأَنَّ ذَلِكَ لَمْ يُدْخِلْهُمْ فِي الإِسْلاَم، وَالدَّلِيلُ قَولُهُ ـــ تَعَالَى ـــ :

﴿ قُلْ مَنْ يَرْزُقُكُمْ مِنَ السَّمَاءِ وَالأَرْضِ أَمَّن يَّمْلِكُ السَّمْعَ وَالأَبْصَارَ وَمَن يُّخْرِجُ الْحَيَّ مِنَ الْمَيِّتِ وَيُخْرِجُ الْمَيِّتَ مِنَ الْحَيِّ وَمَن يُّدَبِّرُ الأَمْرَ فَسَيَقُولُونَ اللهُ فَقُلْ أَفَلا تَتَّقُون ﴾ سورة يونس [٣١-١٠]

القَاعِدَةُ الثّانِيَة

أنَّهُم يَقُولُونَ : مَا دَعَونَاهُم وَتَوَجَّهْنَا إِلَيهِم إلاّ لِطَلَبِ الْقُربَةِ وَالشَّفَاعَة،

فَدَلِيلُ القُرْبَةِ قَولُهُ ـــ تَعَالَى ـــ :

﴿ وَالَّذِينَ اتَّخَذُوا مِنْ دُونِهِ أَولِيَاءَ مَا نَعْبُدُهُمْ إلاّ لِيُقَرِّبُونَا إِلى اللهِ زُلْفَى إِنَّ اللهَ يَحْكُمُ بَيْنَهُمْ فِيمَا هُمْ فِيهِ يَخْتَلِفُونَ إِنَّ اللهَ لا يَهْدِى مَنْ هُوَ كَاذِبٌ كَفَّار ﴾ سورة الزمر [٣-٣٩]

وَدَلِيلُ الشَّفَاعَةِ قَولُهُ ـــ تعالى ـــ :

﴿ وَيَعْبُدُونَ مِنْ دُونِ اللهِ مَا لا يَضُرُّهُمْ وَلا يَنْفَعُهُمْ وَيَقُولُونَ هَؤُلاءِ شُفَعَاؤُنَا عِنْدَ اللهِ ﴾، سورة يونس [١٨-١٠]

وَالشَّفَاعَةُ شَفَاعَتَان : شَفَاعَةٌ مَنْفِيَّة وَشَفَاعَةٌ مُثْبَتَة:

فَالشَّفَاعَةُ المَنْفِيَّةُ مَا كَانَتْ تُطْلَبُ مِنْ غَيْرِ اللهِ فِيمَا لا يَقْدِرُ عَلَيْهِ إلاَّ الله، وَالدَّلِيلُ قَولُهُ ـــ تَعَالى ـــ :

﴿ يَا أَيُّهَا الَّذِينَ آمَنُوا أنفِقُوا مِمَّا رَزَقْنَاكُم مِنْ قَبْلِ أن يَأتِيَ يَوْمٌ لا بَيْعٌ فِيْهِ وَلا خُلَّةٌ وَلا شَفَاعَةٌ وَالْكَافِرُونَ هُمُ الظَّالِمُون ﴾ سورة البقرة [٢٥٤-٢]

وَالشَّفَاعَةُ المُثْبَتَةُ هِيَ : الَّتِي تُطْلَبُ مِنْ اللهِ، وَالشَّافِعُ مُكَرَّمٌ بالشَّفَاعَةِ، وَالمَشْفُوعُ لَهُ : مَنْ رَضِيَ اللهُ قَولَهُ وَعَمَلَهُ بَعْدَ الإذْنِ كَمَا قَالَ ـــ تَعَالَى ـــ :

﴿ مَنْ ذَا الَّذِي يَشْفَعُ عِنْدَهُ إلاَّ بإذْنِه ﴾ سورة البقرة [٢٥٥-٢]

القَاعِدَةُ الثَّالِثَة

أنَّ النَّبيَّ صَلَّى اللهُ عَلَيْهِ وَسَلَّم ظَهَرَ عَلَى أنَاسٍ مُتَفَرِّقِينَ في عِبَادَاتِهِم مِنْهُم مَنْ يَعْبُدُ المَلائِكَة، وَمِنْهُم مَنْ يَعْبُدُ الأنْبِيَاءَ وَالصَّالِحِين، وَمِنْهُم مَنْ يَعْبُدُ الأشْجَار و الأحْجَارَ، وَمِنْهُم مَنْ يَعْبُدُ الشَّمْسَ وَالْقَمَر. وَقَاتَلَهُم رَسُولُ اللهِ صَلَّى اللهُ عَلَيْهِ وَسَلَّمَ وَلَمْ يُفَرِّقْ بَيْنَهُم، وَالدَّلِيلُ قَولُهُ ـــ تَعَالَى ـــ :

﴿ وَقَاتِلُوهُمْ حَتَّى لاَ تَكُونَ فِتْنَةٌ وَيَكُونَ الدِّيْنُ كُلُّهُ لله ﴾ سورة الأنفال [٣٩-٨]

وَدَلِيلُ الشَّمْسِ وَالقَمَرِ قَولُهُ ـــ تَعَالى ـــ :

﴿ وَمِنْ آيَاتِهِ اللَّيْلُ وَالنَّهارُ وَالشَّمْسُ وَالْقَمَرُ لاَ تَسْجُدُوا لِلشَّمْسِ وَلاَ لِلْقَمَرِ ﴾ سورة فصلت [٣٧-٤١]

وَدَلِيْلُ المَلائِكَةِ قَولُهُ ـــ تَعَالى ـــ :

﴿ وَلا يَأمُرَكُمْ أن تَتَّخِذُوا الملائِكَةَ وَالنَّبيِّيْنَ أرْبَابــًا ﴾ الآيَة – سورة آل عمران [٣-٨٠]

وَدَلِيْلُ الأنْبيَاءِ قَولُهُ ــ تَعَالى ــ :

﴿ وَإذْ قَالَ اللهُ يَٰعِيْسَى ابْنَ مَرْيَمَ أأنْتَ قُلْتَ لِلنَّاسِ اتَّخِذُونِي وَأُمِّي إلهَينِ مِنْ دُوْنِ اللهِ قَالَ سُبْحَانَكَ مَا يَكُونُ لي أَنْ أَقُولَ مَا لَيْسَ لي بِحَقٍ إنْ كُنْتُ قُلْتُهُ فَقَدْ عَلِمْتَهُ تَعْلَمُ مَا فِي نَفْسِي وَلا أَعْلَمُ مَا فِي نَفْسِكَ إِنَّكَ أَنْتَ عَلاَّمُ الْغُيُوبِ ﴾ سورة المائدة [٥-١١٦]

وَدَلِيْلُ الصَّالِحِيْنَ قَولُهُ ــ تَعَالى ــ :

﴿ أولئكَ الَّذِيْنَ يَدْعُونَ يَبْتَغُونَ إلى رَبِّهِمُ الْوَسِيْلَةَ أَيُّهُمْ أَقْرَبُ وَيَرْجُونَ رَحْمَتَهُ وَيَخَافُونَ عَذَابَه ... ﴾ الآيَة – سورة الإسراء [١٧-٥٧]

وَدَلِيْلُ الأشْجَار والأحْجَار قَولُهُ ــ تَعَالى ــ :

﴿ أفَرَأيْتُمُ الَّلاَتَ وَالْعُزَّى وَمَنَاةَ الثَّالِثَةَ الأُخْرَى ﴾ سورة النجم [٥٣-١٩-٢٠]

وحَدِيْثُ أبي وَاقِدٍ اللَّيْثِي ــ رَضِيَ اللهُ عَنْهُ ــ قَالَ : خَرَجْنَا مَعَ النَّبيِّ صَلَّى اللهُ عَلَيْهِ وَسَلَّمَ إلَى حُنَيْنٍ وَنَحْنُ حُدَثَاءُ عَهْدٍ بكُفْر، وَلِلْمُشْرِكِيْنَ سِدْرَةٌ يَعْكِفُونَ عِنْدَهَا وَيَنُوطُونَ بهَا أسْلِحَتَهُمْ يُقَالُ لَهَا : ذَاتُ أنْوَاط، فَمَرَرْنَا بسِدْرَةٍ فَقُلْنَا : يَا رَسُولُ اللهِ اجْعَلْ لَنَا ذَاتَ أنْوَاطٍ كَمَا لَهُمْ ذَاتُ أنْوَاط ... الْحَدِيث.

القَاعِدَةُ الرَّابعَة

أنَّ مُشْرِكِي زَمَانِنَا أغْلَظُ شِركــًا مِنَ الأوَّلِين، لأنَّ الأوَّلِيْنَ يُشْرِكُونَ فِي الرَّخَاءِ وَيُخْلِصُونَ فِي الشِّدَّة، وَمُشْرِكُوا زَمَانِنَا شِرْكُهُم دَائِمٌ؛ فِي الرَّخَاءِ

وَالشِّدَّة . وَالدَّلِيلُ قَولُهُ ــ تَعَالى ــ :

﴿ فَإِذَا رَكِبُوا فِي الْفُلْكِ دَعَوُا اللهَ مُخْلِصِيْنَ لَهُ الدِّينَ فَلَمَّا نَجَّاهُمْ إلى الْبَرِّ إِذَا هُمْ يُشْرِكُون ﴾ سورة العنكبوت [٦٥-٢٩]

واللهُ أعلم

وَصَلَّى اللهُ عَلَى مُحَمَّدٍ وَآلِهِ وَصَحْبِهِ وَسَلَّم .

The English Translation of the Text

بِسْمِ ٱللَّهِ ٱلرَّحْمَٰنِ ٱلرَّحِيمِ

In The Name of Allāh, the Ever-Merciful, the Bestower of Mercy

I ask Allāh, the Noble Lord of the Great Throne, that He be your Protector in this world and the Hereafter, and that He makes you blessed wherever you are, and that He makes you from those (people) that, when given, are thankful; and when tested, are patient; and when they sin, they repent. And verily these three are the keys to happiness.

Know, may Allāh guide you to His obedience, that the *ḥanīfiyyah* - the religion of Ibrāhīm - is that you worship Allāh alone, sincerely, making the religion purely for Him. As Allāh, the Most Exalted, says:

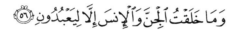

وَمَا خَلَقْتُ ٱلْجِنَّ وَٱلْإِنسَ إِلَّا لِيَعْبُدُونِ ﴿٥٦﴾

"And I did not create the *jinn* and mankind except to worship Me." [Sūrah *Al-Dhāriyāt*, verse 56]

So when you know that Allāh created you to worship Him, then know that 'worship' is not considered worship except with *tawḥīd* (monotheism), like the *ṣalāh* (prayer) is not an acceptable *ṣalāh* except with purity (*ṭahārah*). So if *shirk* enters into worship, it is not accepted, just as impurity destroys purity if it enters into it.

So if you know that when *shirk* is mixed (with worship), the worship is not accepted, and destroys the action, thus making the person acting (upon this kind of worship) from the people who will be permanently in the Hellfire, then you will realise that it is the most important topic for you to study. Perhaps (through this study) Allāh will save you from this evil trap, meaning *shirk* with Allāh, concerning which Allāh - the Exalted - has said:

إِنَّ ٱللَّهَ لَا يَغْفِرُ أَن يُشْرَكَ بِهِۦ وَيَغْفِرُ مَا دُونَ
ذَٰلِكَ لِمَن يَشَآءُ

"Indeed, Allāh does not forgive association (*shirk*) with Him, but He forgives what is less than that for whom He wills." [Sūrah *al-Nisā'*, verse 116]

And this will be (accomplished) through knowing the four principles that Allāh - the Exalted – has mentioned in His book:

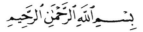

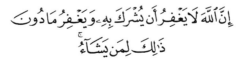

The First Principle

To know that the disbelievers whom the Messenger of Allāh (ﷺ) fought admitted that Allāh - the Exalted - is the Creator, the One who Gives Sustenance, and is in charge of all the affairs, yet this did not enter them into Islām. And the proof is in His, the Exalted's saying:

قُلْ مَن يَرْزُقُكُم
مِّنَ ٱلسَّمَآءِ وَٱلْأَرْضِ أَمَّن يَمْلِكُ ٱلسَّمْعَ وَٱلْأَبْصَٰرَ وَمَن يُخْرِجُ
ٱلْحَىَّ مِنَ ٱلْمَيِّتِ وَيُخْرِجُ ٱلْمَيِّتَ مِنَ ٱلْحَىِّ وَمَن يُدَبِّرُ ٱلْأَمْرَ ۚ
فَسَيَقُولُونَ ٱللَّهُ ۚ فَقُلْ أَفَلَا تَتَّقُونَ ﴿٣١﴾

"Say, 'Who provides for you from the heaven and the earth? Or who controls hearing and the sight and who brings the living out of the dead and brings the dead out of the living and who arranges [every] matter?' They will say, 'Allāh,' so say, 'Then will you not fear Him?'" [Sūrah *Yūnus*, verse 31]

The Second Principle

They (the *mushrikīn*) say, "We do not supplicate to them and turn towards them except to seek nearness and intercession (to Allāh)."

And the proof of the 'nearness' is in His, the Exalted's saying:

وَٱلَّذِينَ ٱتَّخَذُوا۟ مِن دُونِهِۦٓ أَوْلِيَآءَ
مَا نَعْبُدُهُمْ إِلَّا لِيُقَرِّبُونَآ إِلَى ٱللَّهِ زُلْفَىٰٓ إِنَّ ٱللَّهَ يَحْكُمُ بَيْنَهُمْ
فِى مَا هُمْ فِيهِ يَخْتَلِفُونَ ۗ إِنَّ ٱللَّهَ لَا يَهْدِى مَنْ هُوَ كَٰذِبٌ
كَفَّارٌ ﴿٣﴾

"And those who take protectors besides Him [say], 'We only worship them that they may bring us nearer to Allāh in position.' Indeed Allāh will judge between them concerning that over what they differ. Indeed, Allāh does not guide he who is a liar and [confirmed] disbeliever." [Sūrah *al-Zumar*, verse 3]

And the proof of the 'intercession' (*shafāʿah*) is in His, the Exalted's saying:

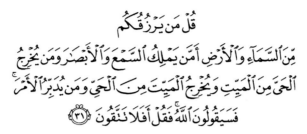

وَيَعْبُدُونَ مِن دُونِ ٱللَّهِ
مَا لَا يَضُرُّهُمْ وَلَا يَنفَعُهُمْ وَيَقُولُونَ هَٰٓؤُلَآءِ شُفَعَٰٓؤُنَا
عِندَ ٱللَّهِ

"And they worship other than Allāh; that which neither harms them nor benefits them, and they say, 'These are our intercessors with Allāh.'" [Sūrah *Yūnus*, verse 18]

And there are two types of intercession: *shafā'ah al-manfiyya* (denied and negated intercession); and *shafā'ah al-muthbata* (affirmed and allowed intercession).

As for *shafā'ah al-manfiyya*, it is what is asked from other than Allāh in which there is no power except that of Allāh's. And the evidence for this is in His, the Exalted's, saying:

يَٰٓأَيُّهَا ٱلَّذِينَ ءَامَنُوٓا۟ أَنفِقُوا۟
مِمَّا رَزَقْنَٰكُم مِّن قَبْلِ أَن يَأْتِىَ يَوْمٌ لَّا بَيْعٌ فِيهِ وَلَا خُلَّةٌ وَلَا
شَفَٰعَةٌ ۗ وَٱلْكَٰفِرُونَ هُمُ ٱلظَّٰلِمُونَ ﴿٢٥٤﴾

"O you who believe! Spend from that which We have provided for you before there comes a Day in which there is no exchange [i.e. ransom] and no friendship and no intercession. And the disbelievers are the wrongdoers." [Sūrah *al-Baqarah*, verse 254]

And *shafā'ah al-muthbata* is that which is asked from Allāh. The one performing the intercession is honoured (by Allāh) due to the intercession. And the one being interceded for is one whom Allāh is pleased with his sayings and his actions. (The *shafā'ah al-muthbata* occurs) after permission (from Allāh is given), as the Most Exalted says:

مَن ذَا ٱلَّذِى يَشْفَعُ عِندَهُۥٓ إِلَّا بِإِذْنِهِۦ

"Who is there that can intercede with Him, except by His permission?" [Sūrah *al-Baqarah*, verse 255]

The Third Principle

That the Prophet (ﷺ) came to the people who had different (objects) of worship: from them are the worshippers of the angels. And from them are the worshippers of the prophets and the pious. And from them are the worshippers of the trees and the stones. And from them are the worshippers of the sun and the moon. But the Messenger of Allāh (ﷺ) fought them all, and did not consider the differences between them.

And the proof of this is in His, the Exalted's, saying:

وَقَٰتِلُوهُمْ حَتَّىٰ
لَا تَكُونَ فِتْنَةٌ وَيَكُونَ ٱلدِّينُ كُلُّهُۥ لِلَّهِ ۚ

"And fight them until there is no *fitnah* (tribulations) and [until] the religion [i.e., worship], all of it, is for Allāh." [Sūrah *al-Anfāl*, verse 39]

And the proof of (worshipping) the sun and the moon is His saying:

وَمِنْ ءَايَٰتِهِ
ٱلَّيْلُ وَٱلنَّهَارُ وَٱلشَّمْسُ وَٱلْقَمَرُ ۚ لَا تَسْجُدُوا۟ لِلشَّمْسِ
وَلَا لِلْقَمَرِ وَٱسْجُدُوا۟ لِلَّهِ ٱلَّذِى خَلَقَهُنَّ إِن كُنتُمْ
إِيَّاهُ تَعْبُدُونَ ﴿٣٧﴾

"And from His signs are the night and the day, and the sun and the moon. Do not prostrate to the sun or to the moon, but prostrate to Allāh, who created them, if it should be Him that you worship." [Sūrah *Fuṣṣilat*, verse 37]

And the proof of (worshipping) the angels is in His, the Exalted's, saying:

وَلَا يَأْمُرَكُمْ أَن تَتَّخِذُوا۟ ٱلْمَلَٰٓئِكَةَ وَٱلنَّبِيِّۦنَ أَرْبَابًا ۗ

"And they (the prophets of Allāh) did not order that you take the angels and the prophets as gods." [Sūrah *Āl-ʿImrān*, verse 80]

And the proof of (worshipping) the prophets is in His, the Exalted's, saying:

وَإِذْ قَالَ ٱللَّهُ يَٰعِيسَى ٱبْنَ مَرْيَمَ ءَأَنتَ قُلْتَ لِلنَّاسِ ٱتَّخِذُونِى
وَأُمِّىَ إِلَٰهَيْنِ مِن دُونِ ٱللَّهِ ۖ قَالَ سُبْحَٰنَكَ مَا يَكُونُ لِىٓ أَنْ
أَقُولَ مَا لَيْسَ لِى بِحَقٍّ ۚ إِن كُنتُ قُلْتُهُۥ فَقَدْ عَلِمْتَهُۥ ۚ تَعْلَمُ مَا فِى
نَفْسِى وَلَآ أَعْلَمُ مَا فِى نَفْسِكَ ۚ إِنَّكَ أَنتَ عَلَّٰمُ ٱلْغُيُوبِ ﴿١١٦﴾

"And [beware of the Day] when Allāh will say, 'O Jesus, Son of Mary, did you say to the people, "Take me and my mother as deities besides Allāh?"' He will say, 'Exalted are You! It was not for me to say what I have no right (to say). If I had said it, You would have known it. You know what is within myself, and

I do not know what is within Yourself. Indeed, it is You who is Knower of the unseen.'" [Sūrah *al-Mā'idah*, verse 116]

And the proof of (worshipping) the pious is in His, the Exalted's, saying:

أُولَٰٓئِكَ ٱلَّذِينَ
يَدْعُونَ يَبْتَغُونَ إِلَىٰ رَبِّهِمُ ٱلْوَسِيلَةَ أَيُّهُمْ أَقْرَبُ وَيَرْجُونَ
رَحْمَتَهُۥ وَيَخَافُونَ عَذَابَهُۥٓ

"Those whom they invoke (besides Allāh are themselves) seeking a means of access to their Lord, (striving as to) which of them would be nearest, hoping for His Mercy and fearing His punishment." [Sūrah *al-Isrā'*, verse 57]

And the proof of the (worshipping) of the trees and the stones is in His, the Exalted's, saying:

أَفَرَءَيْتُمُ ٱللَّٰتَ وَٱلْعُزَّىٰ ﴿١٩﴾ وَمَنَوٰةَ ٱلثَّالِثَةَ ٱلْأُخْرَىٰٓ ﴿٢٠﴾

"So have you considered al-Lāt and al-'Uzzā? And Manāt, the third - the other one?" [Sūrah *al-Najm*, verses 19-20]

And (another proof is) the ḥadīth of Abī Wāqid al-Laythī (*raḍiyallāhu 'anhu*), in which he said: "We left with the Prophet (ﷺ) to Ḥunayn, and at the time we were close to the period of *kufr* (disbelief). And the pagans had a place of worship upon which they hung their weapons. It was called, '*Dhāt Anwāṭ*.' So when we passed by that place of worship, we said: "O Messenger of Allāh, make for us a place of hanging like they have a place of hanging...."

The Fourth Principle

That the *mushriks* of our time are more severe in *shirk* than those of before, because those of the past committed *shirk* in (times of) ease, but were sincere (to Allāh) in (times of) hardship. However, the *mushriks* of our time are always committing *shirk*, in ease and in hardship. The evidence for this is in His, the Most Exalted's saying:

فَإِذَا رَكِبُوا۟ فِى
ٱلْفُلْكِ دَعَوُا۟ ٱللَّهَ مُخْلِصِينَ لَهُ ٱلدِّينَ فَلَمَّا نَجَّىٰهُمْ إِلَى ٱلْبَرِّ إِذَا
هُمْ يُشْرِكُونَ ﴿٦٥﴾

"And when they board a ship, they supplicate to Allāh, making the religion sincere to Him. But when He delivers them to the land, at once they associate others with Him." [Sūrah *al-ʿAnkabūt*, verse 65]

And Allāh knows best, and may the extolation and peace of Allāh be upon Muḥammad, and his family and his companions.

The Explanation of The Four Principles of *Shirk*

Introduction

TEXT

بسم الله الرحمن الرحيم

أسأَلُ اللهَ الكَرِيمَ رَبَّ العَرْشِ العَظِيمِ أن يَتَوَلَّاكَ في الدُّنيا وَالآخِرَة، وَأن يَجْعَلَكَ مُبَارَكًا أيْنَمَا كُنْتَ، وَأن يَجْعَلَكَ مِمَّن إذا أُعْطِيَ شَكَرَ، وَإذَا ابْتُلِيَ صَبَرَ، وَإذَا أذْنَبَ اسْتَغْفَر، فَإنَّ هَذِهِ الثَّلاثَ عُنْوَانُ السَّعَادَة.

In the name of Allāh, the Most Merciful, the Bestower of Mercy

> I ask Allāh, the Noble Lord of the Great Throne, that He be your Protector in this world and the Hereafter, and that He makes you blessed wherever you are, and that He makes you from those (people) that, when given, are thankful; and when tested, are patient; and when they sin, they repent. And verily these three are the keys to happiness.

EXPLANATION The Shaykh starts his work with the *basmalah*, or the phrase *Bismillāh al-Rahmān al-Rahīm*. By this, he follows the sunnah of Allāh and His Messenger. For Allāh started the first Sūrah in the Qur'ān with the *āyah*: *Bismillāh al-Rahmān al-Rahīm*. And He started every single Sūrah with the *basmalah* except for Sūrah *al-Tawbah*. And the Prophet (ﷺ) also used to start his letters with the *basmalah*. When he (ﷺ) wrote a letter to Heraclius, the Caesar of Rome, it stated:

> *Bismillāh al-Rahmān al-Rahīm*. From Muḥammad, the worshipper of Allāh and His Messenger, to Heraclius, the leader of the Romans.[14]

There are many benefits of reciting the *basmalah* before any act. Firstly, one follows the sunnah of Allāh and His Messenger, as has preceded. Secondly, he reminds himself that the purpose of this act – whatever it might be – is that he gain the reward of Allāh by doing it. Even a non-religious act, if done with the proper intentions, can be rewarded by Allāh, as long as the act itself and the reason that it is performed are permissible. Thirdly, it is an implicit *du'ā* to Allāh to bless him in this act, and cause him to be successful in it. Fourthly, when a person develops the habit of saying the *basmalah*, he will automatically decrease in his sins. This is because he will unconsciously say the *basmalah* before every act that he does, so if that act is a sin, he will remind himself of Allāh, and avoid performing the act.

[14] Reported by al-Bukhārī, (# 7). For the remainder of the letter, the reader is referred to al-Bukhārī.

The author then makes a sincere *du'ā* for the reader, and this is indicative of his concern for the Muslims, for he prays that Allāh protect the reader from all harm, and that He make him blessed wherever he may be. One of the primary ways that a person will be blessed is by gaining knowledge, and then spreading it wherever he goes. Thus, people will benefit from him at all times and locations, and he will spread good wherever he goes. This same *du'ā* was made by the noble prophet 'Īsa ibn Maryam, who said while he was still a baby in his cradle,

وَجَعَلَنِي مُبَارَكًا أَيْنَ مَا كُنتُ

And He has made me blessed wheresoever I be.[15]

The author also uses the lofty Names and Attributes of Allāh to draw closer to Him in order for his *du'ās* to be accepted, for he states that he is praying to Allāh '...the Lord of the Noble Throne.' The Throne of Allāh is one of the greatest Signs of Allāh. It is the largest creation, for no created object is larger than it, or heavier than it. It has pillars which distinguished angels hold. It also has angels that surround it, who continually praise Allāh, and seek forgiveness for the believers. It is the highest of all created objects, and the roof of *Jannat al-Firdaws.*[16] It has been described in the Qur'ān with the term *majīd*, which implies that it is a majestic and noble Throne, and also with the term *'adhīm*, which signifies that it is a great and massive Throne. And it is this great Throne over which Allāh Himself has Risen, as He has said in over seven verses of the Qur'ān:

ٱلرَّحْمَٰنُ عَلَى ٱلْعَرْشِ ٱسْتَوَىٰ ﴿٥﴾

The *Rahmān* (Ever-Merciful) has risen over the Throne.[17]

All of these attributes of the Throne are authentically narrated in the Qur'ān and ḥadith. So the author uses the title 'The Noble Lord of the Throne,' in order to increase the possibility of his *du'ā* being accepted.

The Shaykh mentions three characteristics that he calls the 'keys to happiness,' since any person who has been blessed with these keys will be able to open up the doors of good and happiness in this world and the Hereafter. This is because every matter that occurs to a believer is either something that he desires, or something that is undesirable and brings evil consequences. So a matter that is desirable is without a doubt a blessing from Allāh, and as such necessitates that a servant be thankful to Allāh for such a blessing. Allāh states in the Qur'ān:

---

[15] Sūrah *Maryam*, verse 31.

[16] *Jannat al-Firdaws* is the highest level of Paradise; may Allāh make it our place of abode!

[17] Sūrah *Ṭā Hā*, verse 5.

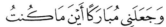

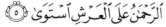

مَآ أَصَابَكَ مِنْ حَسَنَةٍ فَمِنَ ٱللَّهِ

And whatever good occurs to you is from Allāh.[18]

And He also states:

لَئِن شَكَرْتُمْ لَأَزِيدَنَّكُمْ

If you give thanks, I will increase (your good).[19]

True thanks to Allāh entails a physical thanking, such as with the phrase: *Alḥamdulillāh*. It also entails not abusing or misusing the good fortunes that Allāh has blessed a person with. Rather, true gratefulness to Allāh necessitates that one uses the blessings that he has to worship Allāh even more. So, for example, if a person wishes to thank Allāh for the money that he has been blessed with, this is achieved by paying *zakāt* on this money, and by using it to gain the pleasure of Allāh.

If some misfortune occurs to a servant, then this misfortune is either a religious one that he has caused himself – and this is called a sin, or is a worldly misfortune that occurs with the Will of Allāh – and this is a test and trial from Allāh. So when a Muslim commits a sin, he realises the error of what he has done, and tries to correct it immediately by repenting from the sin. Allāh states,

إِنَّمَا ٱلتَّوْبَةُ عَلَى ٱللَّهِ لِلَّذِينَ يَعْمَلُونَ ٱلسُّوٓءَ بِجَهَٰلَةٍ
ثُمَّ يَتُوبُونَ مِن قَرِيبٍ فَأُو۟لَٰٓئِكَ يَتُوبُ ٱللَّهُ عَلَيْهِمْ ۗ وَكَانَ
ٱللَّهُ عَلِيمًا حَكِيمًا ﴿١٧﴾

Verily, repentance that Allāh accepts are from those who commit a sin ignorantly (and foolishly), and then repent immediately. So as for these people, Allāh will accept their repentance, and indeed, Allāh is Ever-Knowing, All-Wise.[20]

True repentance must be done sincerely for the sake of Allāh. It must accompany a genuine feeling of guilt, and an earnest determination not to return to the sin. Additionally, the sinner must increase in his asking for forgiveness from Allāh, and his good deeds, so that Allāh might wipe away the evil that he has done.

---

[18] Sūrah *al-Nisā'*, verse 79.

[19] Sūrah *Ibrāhīm*, verse 7.

[20] Sūrah *al-Nisā'*, verse 17.

As for a worldly misfortune, then a person should be fully aware that the life of this world is merely a testing ground, during which he will be afflicted with many types of adversities, to see whether he is thankful or not. Allāh states,

وَلَنَبْلُوَنَّكُم بِشَيْءٍ مِّنَ ٱلْخَوْفِ وَٱلْجُوعِ
وَنَقْصٍ مِّنَ ٱلْأَمْوَٰلِ وَٱلْأَنفُسِ وَٱلثَّمَرَٰتِ ۗ وَبَشِّرِ ٱلصَّـٰبِرِينَ
﴿١٥٥﴾ ٱلَّذِينَ إِذَآ أَصَـٰبَتْهُم مُّصِيبَةٌ قَالُوٓا۟ إِنَّا لِلَّهِ وَإِنَّآ إِلَيْهِ رَٰجِعُونَ

> And of a surety We will test you, with fear, and hunger, and a loss of money, and life, and fruits; and give glad tidings to those who are patient. Those whom, when an affliction falls on them, say, 'Verily, to Allāh we belong, and to Him we will return.'[21]

So whoever is able to thank Allāh for the good that he has been blessed with, repent to Allāh for the sins that he has done, and be patient for the sake of Allāh whenever a misfortune befalls him, has indeed been granted the keys to all good fortune.

Worship: Goals and Definition

TEXT

اعْلَمْ ــ أرْشَدَكَ اللهُ لِطَاعَتِهِ ــ : أنَّ الْحَنِيْفِيَّةَ مِلَّةَ إبْراهِيمَ : أنْ تَعْبُدَ اللهَ وَحْدَهُ مُخْلِصـاً لَهُ الدِّيْنَ كَمَا قَالَ ــ تَعَالَى ــ

﴿ وَمَا خَلَقْتُ الْجِنَّ وَالإنْسَ إلاّ لِيَعْبُدُونِ ﴾ سورة الذاريات [٥٦-٥١]

> Know – may Allāh guide you to His obedience – that the *ḥanīfiyyah* – the religion of Ibrāhīm – is that you worship Allāh alone, sincerely, making the religion purely for Him. As Allāh, the Most Exalted, says: "And I did not create the *jinn* and mankind except to worship Me." [Sūrah *al-Dhāriyāt*, verse 56]

EXPLANATION

The author defines the religion of the great Prophet Ibrāhīm. Ibrāhīm *alayhi as-salām* is one of the greatest of all the prophets, and one who is respected by all those who claim to worship Allāh. If one looks at the religion of Ibrāhīm, he finds that it was the pure worship of Allāh. Allāh states,

---

[21] Sūrah *al-Baqarah*, verse 156.

مَا كَانَ إِبْرَٰهِيمُ يَهُودِيًّا وَلَا نَصْرَانِيًّا وَلَٰكِن كَانَ حَنِيفًا مُّسْلِمًا

Ibrāhīm was neither a Jew, nor a Christian, but rather he was a *ḥanīf*, submitting (himself to Allāh).[22]

And in another verse, He says,

وَمَنْ أَحْسَنُ دِينًا مِّمَّنْ أَسْلَمَ وَجْهَهُۥ لِلَّهِ وَهُوَ مُحْسِنٌ وَاتَّبَعَ مِلَّةَ إِبْرَٰهِيمَ حَنِيفًا

And who has a better religion than he who submits himself to Allāh (in Islām), and is righteous, and follows the religion of Ibrāhīm, the *ḥanīf*?[23]

The term *ḥanīf* means that a person inclines himself to the worship of Allāh, and leaves everything besides Allāh by turning away from *shirk*. That is why the people who rejected the idol-worship of the Arabs, but lived before the time of the Prophet (ﷺ), were called *ḥanīfs*, as they would turn away from such idolatry, and instead worship Allāh alone.

Once, the Prophet (ﷺ) was asked, "Which religion is the most beloved to Allāh?" So he replied,

"The gentle *ḥanīfiyyah*,"[24]

which is the religion of Islām. So in this ḥadīth he called Islām the 'gentle *ḥanīfiyyah*,' signifying that it is the essence of the religion of Ibrāhīm, which was the pure worship of Allāh.

Allāh states, in the verse quoted by the author, the purpose of creation. This verse is absolutely explicit in stating the true purpose of creation, and that is so that mankind and *jinn* may worship Allāh. Therefore, it is imperative that the concept and definition of worship is discussed, in order for a person to understand the purpose of creation.

Linguistically, worship – or *'ibādah* – is defined as having a complete love for the object that is worshipped, along with complete humility and servitude.[25] So when an object is loved, but a person does not feel humble towards it, then this is not known as *'ibādah*. Such an instance might occur when a father shows love

---

[22] Sūrah *Āl-'Imrān*, verse 67.

[23] Sūrah *al-Nisā'*, verse 125.

[24] Reported by al-Bukhārī in his *al-Adab al-Mufrad*, (# 387). (See *al-Ṣaḥīḥah*, # 881).

[25] See *Mukhtaṣar al-Ṣiḥāḥ*, of al-Rāzi, p. 408.

towards his family and children. Likewise, when an object is shown servitude and humbleness, without any love, this too is not known as worship. Such an instance might occur with a ruler or a king. Only when these two characteristics are combined in their fullest form will *'ibādah* take place.

When the term *'ibādah* occurs in the texts of the Qur'ān or sunnah, it refers to a wide range of actions that includes all actions and statements that Allāh loves and is pleased with, whether these actions are actions of the heart, the tongue or the limbs.[26] So, for example, *'ibādah* of the heart includes loving Allāh, fearing Allāh, and hoping the best from Allāh; *'ibādah* of the tongue includes reciting the Qur'ān, remembering Allāh, and calling others to the worship of Allāh; and *'ibādah* of the limbs includes fasting, praying and giving charity. So it can be seen that the term *'ibādah* is a very wide and vast term, since it includes all actions that Allāh commands and is pleased with.

'Ibādah has two basic pre-conditions to it, and three pillars. The term 'pre-conditions' signifies that every single act of worship that is performed must meet these two simple conditions in order for the act to be accepted. No act qualifies as an act of worship until these two conditions are met. The term 'pillar' signifies that these pillars must be present when the act is performed, in order for it to be a perfect act of worship.

The first pre-condition is that the act be done solely for the sake of Allāh. This is the essence of *tawḥīd* – that all of a person's actions be solely for the sake of Allāh. And this is the implementation of the phrase: *Lā ilāha illa Allāh*, which is the first half of the testimony of faith. By affirming that there is no deity that is worthy of worship besides Allāh, a person affirms that all of his religious acts will be done solely for Allāh's sake.

The second pre-condition is that the act that is performed be in accordance with the Prophet's (ﷺ) sunnah. In other words, a person cannot invent an act of worship by himself, for the only way to know whether a particular act is an act of worship or not is to see if the Prophet (ﷺ) commanded it or not. And this is the actualisation of the phrase: *Muḥammadur Rasūl Allāh*, the second half of the testimony of faith. By affirming that Muḥammad (ﷺ) is the true Messenger and Prophet of Allāh, a person affirms that only the Prophet (ﷺ) has the right to be obeyed totally and without question. The only person that can inform us of how to worship Allāh is the Prophet (ﷺ), since he is the one who Allāh communicates with.

Fuḍayl ibn 'Iyāḍ[27] said in reference to the verse:

---

[26] *Majmū' al-Fatāwa*, (10/149).

[27] Fuḍayl ibn 'Iyāḍ ibn Ma'sūd al-Timīmi (187 A.H.) was born in Samarqand, and grew up to be a highway robber. However, he repented from this, and travelled to Kūfah in search of knowledge. He became well known for his abstinence and piety. cf. *Tahzīb al-Kamāl* (4763); *Tahzīb al-Tahzīb* (5647).

لِيَبْلُوَكُمْ أَيُّكُمْ أَحْسَنُ عَمَلًا

"That He may test you which of you is best in deeds."[28]

"(This means the deeds that are done) correctly and with a sincere intention. If a deed is done sincerely, yet incorrectly, it will not be accepted, and likewise, if a deed is done correctly but insincerely, it will also be rejected. Only when a deed is done *correctly* and *sincerely* will it be accepted. And '*sincerity*' means to perform a deed solely for the sake of Allah, and '*correctly*' means to perform it upon the sunnah."[29]

So these two pre-requisites are essential before a person starts any act of worship. If the first pre-condition is not met, then the act will be considered a type of *shirk*, since it was done for other than Allāh. And if the second pre-condition is not met, then the act will be considered an innovation, or *bid' ah*.

At the same time, there are three essential pillars upon which all of a person's worship is based. In other words, while he or she is performing any act of worship, these three pillars must be present in order for it to be a complete and perfect act. It can also be stated that these three pillars are in fact the *driving force* for all acts of worship.

These three pillars are: love, fear, and hope. So a person worships Allāh out of a love for Allāh, and a fear for Allāh's punishment, and a sincere hope for gaining Allāh's reward. If any of these three conditions is not met, then the proper *spirit* of worship will not be present.

Some of the scholars gave an example of *'ibādah* and these three pillars in the form of a bird with its two wings. The heart of the bird is the love of Allāh, and 'fear' and 'hope' are its two wings. So if the 'love' (the heart) is not present, the *'ibādah* (the bird) will be completely dead. And if either 'hope' or 'fear' is absent, the *'ibādah* will not be able to move.

Although the evidences for each of these three pillars are numerous, Allāh combines them in one verse that is also mentioned later by the author:

أُولَٰئِكَ الَّذِينَ
يَدْعُونَ يَبْتَغُونَ إِلَىٰ رَبِّهِمُ الْوَسِيلَةَ أَيُّهُمْ أَقْرَبُ وَيَرْجُونَ
رَحْمَتَهُ وَيَخَافُونَ عَذَابَهُ

---

[28] Sūrah *al-Mulk*, verse 2.

[29] *Jami' al-' Ulūm*, p. 59.

"Those whom they invoke (besides Allāh) seek a means of closeness to their Lord, (striving as to) which of them would be nearest, hoping for His Mercy and fearing His punishment."[30]

In this verse, Allāh describes the situation of His servants who are worshipped by ignorant people. These servants are racing with one another, trying to come close to Allāh, because they love Him. At the same time, they are hopeful of achieving Allāh's Mercy, and fearful of His punishment. So they worship Allāh based on the three pillars of love, fear and hope.

Tawḥīd and *Shirk*

فَإِذَا عَرَفْتَ أَنَّ اللهَ خَلَقَكَ لِعِبَادَتِهِ فَاعْلَمْ : أَنَّ الْعِبَادَةَ لاَ تُسَمَّى عِبَادَةً إِلاَّ مَعَ التَّوْحِيدِ، كَمَا أَنَّ الصَّلاةَ لا تُسَمَّى صَلاَةً إلاّ مَعَ الطَّهَارَةِ، فَإِذَا دَخَلَ الشِّرْكُ فِي العِبَادَةِ فَسَدَتْ كَالحَدَثِ إذا دَخَلَ في الطَّهارَة. TEXT

So when you know that Allāh created you to worship Him, then know that 'worship' is not considered worship except with *tawḥīd* (monotheism), like the *ṣalāh* (prayer) is not an acceptable *ṣalāh* except with purity (*ṭahārah*). So if *shirk* enters into worship, it is not accepted, just as impurity destroys purity if it enters into it.

The worship of Allāh has two necessary pre-conditions to it, as has preceded, the first of which is *sincerity*. This means that acts of worship are directed only to Allāh. This is the crux of *tawḥīd*, which is the message of all the prophets of Allāh. *Tawḥīd* is defined as: the singling out of Allāh in worship, while believing in His Unique Essence, Attributes, and Actions. EXPLANAT.

So there are two aspects of *tawḥīd*. The first aspect deals with the conceptual perception of the Essence of the Creator. A person must affirm the perfect existence of Allāh, and consider His Essence, Names and Attributes to be Unique and Perfect. This aspect is known in Arabic as *Tawḥīd al-ʿItiqādī*, meaning '*Tawḥīd* in one's beliefs.' The second aspect deals with the actualisation of this affirmation, by unifying the goal of all acts of worship to be the pleasure of Allāh. This aspect is known as *Tawḥīd al-ʿAmalī*, or '*Tawḥīd* in one's actions.'

These two aspects are equally essential in order for a person's *tawḥīd* to be complete. So, for example, if someone believes that Allāh has a son, but directs all acts of worship to Allāh alone, he is not a Muslim. Likewise, if he believes in the perfect Existence of Allāh, but directs his acts of worship to an idol, he is not

---

[30] Sūrah *al-Isrā'*, verse 57.

a Muslim. Only when a person affirms and practices *tawḥīd* in its full sense will he be a Muslim.

Shirk is the antithesis of *tawḥīd*. It is not possible for *tawḥīd* to exist alongside with *shirk* in the heart of a person. *Shirk* is defined as: taking a partner with Allāh. In other words, it entails giving a right that is due to Allāh to a created object instead. So if a person enters into *shirk*, he automatically exits from *tawḥīd*, since *tawḥīd*, by its very definition, is the purifying of one's actions for the sake of Allāh. The example that the author gives helps clarify this point. Just like an act that breaks a person's ablution nullifies it, no matter how little or small that act is, likewise, *shirk* destroys a person's *tawḥīd*, no matter how small or insignificant it might seem.

Therefore, if a person falls into *shirk*, all of his actions will be rejected.

Allāh states in the Qur'ān,

وَلَقَدْ أُوحِيَ إِلَيْكَ وَإِلَى الَّذِينَ مِن قَبْلِكَ لَئِنْ
أَشْرَكْتَ لَيَحْبَطَنَّ عَمَلُكَ وَلَتَكُونَنَّ مِنَ الْخَاسِرِينَ ﴿٦٥﴾

> And it has indeed been inspired to you, and to (the prophets) before you, that if you commit *shirk*, then all of your deeds will be destroyed, and you will be amongst the losers.[31]

In this verse, Allāh states that even if the Prophet (ﷺ) were to fall into *shirk* – and of course this is not possible – then all of his good deeds would go to waste, and not be accepted by Allāh. In this there is a severe warning against *shirk*, for it destroys all of a person's good deeds, just like if a person were to break his *wuḍu*, it would destroy his entire *ṣalāt*.

Importance of Knowing *Shirk*

TEXT

فَإذا عَرَفْتَ أَنَّ الشِّركَ إذا خالَطَ العِبادَةَ أفسدَها وَأحبطَ العَمَلَ وَصارَ صاحِبُهُ مِنَ الْخالِدِيْنَ فِي النّار عَرَفْتَ أنَّ أهَمَّ ما عَلَيكَ : مَعْرِفَةُ ذَلِكَ، لَعَلَّ اللهَ أنْ يُخَلِّصَكَ مِنْ هَذه الشَّبَكَةِ، وَهِيَ الشِّرْكُ باللهِ الَّذي قالَ اللهُ تَعالَى فِيه:

﴿ إنَّ اللهَ لا يَغْفِرُ أنْ يُشْرَكَ بِهِ وَيَغْفِرُ ما دُوْنَ ذَلِكَ لِمَنْ يَشاء ﴾ سورة النساء [٤-١١٦]

[31] Sūrah *al-Zumar*, verse 65.

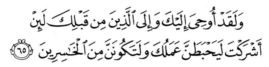

وَذَلِكَ بِمَعْرِفَةِ أَرْبَعَةِ قَوَاعِدَ ذَكَرَهَا اللهُ ـــ تَعَالَى ـــ فِي كِتَابِهِ

So if you know that when *shirk* is mixed (with worship), the worship is not accepted, and destroys the action, thus making the person acting (upon this kind of worship) from the people who will be permanently in the Hellfire, then you will realise that it is the most important topic for you to study. Perhaps (through this study) Allāh will save you from this evil trap, meaning *shirk* with Allāh, concerning which Allāh - the Exalted – has said:

"Indeed, Allāh does not forgive association with Him, but He forgives what is less than that for whom He wills." [Sūrah *al-Nisā'*, verse 116]

And this will be (accomplished) through knowing the four principles that Allāh the Exalted has mentioned in His Book.

EXPLANATI

The importance of studying any matter is dependent on its potential benefit or harm. Therefore, we find that many disciplines of science aim at procuring benefit for man, such as engineering. Likewise, we find doctors who spend their entire lives studying various diseases, not so that they can be affected by it, but rather to learn its dangers, and thus prevent the occurrence or spread of these diseases.

It is with this perspective in mind that we find Islām actually commands us to learn and study certain evils. Allāh says in the Qur'ān:

وَكَذَٰلِكَ نُفَصِّلُ ٱلْآيَٰتِ وَلِتَسْتَبِينَ سَبِيلُ ٱلْمُجْرِمِينَ ﴿٥٥﴾

And this is how We explain the Signs, and so that the path of the criminals is made clear.[32]

So Allāh has made clear the path of the believer, and *He has also made clear the path of the criminals* (who are all those who oppose the path of the believers), and by doing so, the one traversing these paths will be better able to distinguish between the two, and thus save himself from danger. That is why Ḥudayfah ibn al-Yamān, one of the great Companions, said, "The Companions would ask the Prophet (ﷺ) about good matters, but I would ask him about evil matters, for I was fearful that they might fall upon me."[33] And ʿUmar ibn al-Khaṭṭāb said, "The pillars of Islām will be destroyed, one by one, when people who do not know *Jāhilīyyah*[34] are raised in Islām."[35] The meaning of this profound statement

---

[32] Sūrah *al-Anʿām*, verse 55.

[33] Reported by Muslim, (# 4726).

[34] The term *Jāhilīyyah* literally means 'ignorance.' It is used to describe the time period before the advent of the Prophet (ﷺ), as mankind was in a state of ignorance with regards to Allāh. The term also refers to all types of evil.

[35] *Taysīr al-ʿAzīz al-Ḥamīd*, p. 83.

is that when people do not realise how to recognise evil, they will fall into it. One of the reasons that the Companions were the best of this nation was that they were raised in the worst of all *Jāhilīyyah*, so when Islām came, they became the purest of the pure. Due to the evil that they were raised in, they appreciated the purity of Islām in a manner that others who are raised in Islām will not understand. It is because of this that the Companions realised the meanings and implications of *shirk* and *tawḥīd*, and therefore did not exaggerate in the status of the prophets and saints like the Muslims of later generations did.

So knowledge of evil is a very important factor in perfecting one's belief. Like the poet versified:

Learn evil, not for the sake of evil, but rather to avoid it.

For verily, he who does not know evil from good will fall into it.

If a person realises that the sin of *shirk* is the greatest sin and the biggest evil, and is the one sin that Allāh has promised not to forgive, then he will realise the great importance of studying *shirk*. Only by studying *shirk* will a person grasp the perils that he might fall into by committing *shirk*. Also, once a person realises how dangerous *shirk* is, he will study its various types and forms, for the knowledge of how dangerous a matter is, is not sufficient to protect yourself from it. It is also imperative that a person be able to recognise its existence, and the signs of *shirk*, and its symptoms. He must also be aware of the factors that help him avoid *shirk* and protect him from falling into it. And he must be prepared to defend his position in front of others who are committing *shirk*, so that he can establish the evidence upon them, and call them to the pure *tawḥīd* of Allāh. He must also study the reasons and false evidences that those who commit *shirk* use to justify *shirk*, so that he can refute them and be more effective in his calling to the pure worship of Allāh. And all of this can only be accomplished by a detailed study of *shirk*, and all factors related to it.

Some of the grave consequences of *shirk* are:

- It is the only sin that Allāh has promised He will never forgive, and the proof for this is mentioned by the author.
- The one who commits *shirk* has prohibited himself from entering Paradise, and obligated for himself Hell as his permanent abode, as Allāh says:

إِنَّهُۥ مَن يُشْرِكْ بِٱللَّهِ فَقَدْ حَرَّمَ ٱللَّهُ عَلَيْهِ
ٱلْجَنَّةَ وَمَأْوَىٰهُ ٱلنَّارُ

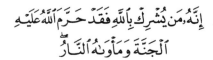

> Whoever commits *shirk* with Allāh, then Allāh has made Paradise prohibited for him, and his abode will be in the Fire.[36]

- The person who commits *shirk* destroys all of his good deeds, so that none of them will be accepted by Allāh, as has been mentioned in a preceding verse.
- The matter that has been prohibited the most in the Qur'ān is that of *shirk*. There are literally hundreds of verses in which Allāh has directly or indirectly warned against *shirk*, and no other matter has been warned against so severely.

So can their be a matter that is more dangerous and evil than *shirk*? Therefore, when one realises these dangers, he will strive – by studying *shirk* – to avoid it.

The author states that the knowledge of *shirk* can be obtained from studying '...the four principles.' From the phrase, '*...the four principles*,' the title of the book is taken. These four principles explain and clarify the precise meaning of *shirk*, and are based on the Qur'ān and sunnah, and on the history of the Arabs before Islām. Of course, this does not imply that these four principles are the *only* knowledge that one needs to understand *shirk*, but rather that these principles are a sufficient introduction to understand the basic concepts of *shirk*.

The First Principle القَاعِدَةُ الأُولَى

TEXT

أَنْ تَعْلَمَ أَنَّ الْكُفَّارَ الَّذِينَ قَاتَلَهُمْ رَسُولُ اللهِ صَلَّى اللهُ عَلَيْهِ وَسَلَّمَ يُقِرُّونَ بِأَنَّ اللهَ ـــ تَعَالَى ـــ هُوَ الْخَالِقُ الرَّازِقُ الْمُدَبِّرُ، وَأَنَّ ذَلِكَ لَمْ يُدْخِلْهُمْ فِي الإِسْلَامِ، وَالدَّلِيلُ قَوْلُهُ ـــ تَعَالَى ـــ :

﴿ قُلْ مَنْ يَرْزُقُكُمْ مِنَ السَّمَاءِ وَالأَرْضِ أَمَّنْ يَمْلِكُ السَّمْعَ وَالأَبْصَارَ وَمَنْ يُخْرِجُ الْحَيَّ مِنَ الْمَيِّتِ وَيُخْرِجُ الْمَيِّتَ مِنَ الْحَيِّ وَمَنْ يُدَبِّرُ الأَمْرَ فَسَيَقُولُونَ اللهُ فَقُلْ أَفَلَا تَتَّقُونَ ﴾ سورة يونس [١٠-٣١]

To know that the disbelievers whom the Messenger of Allāh (ﷺ) fought admitted that Allāh – the Exalted – is the Creator, the One who Gives Sustenance, and the One who is in charge of all the affairs, yet this did not enter them into Islām. And the proof is in His, the Exalted's saying:

---

[36] Sūrah *al-Mā'idah*, verse 72.

Say, "Who provides for you from the heaven and the earth? Or who controls hearing and the sight, and who brings the living out of the dead, and brings the dead out of the living, and who arranges [every] matter?" They will say, 'Allāh,' so say, 'Then will you not fear Him?'" [Sūrah *Yūnus*, verse 31]

EXPLANATION This principle is an extremely important principle, and its ignorance has caused many people to go astray. Yet, its evidences are so many, and its proofs so clear, that there is no room for doubt concerning it.

The Arabs that opposed the message of the Prophet (ﷺ), and fought against him, used to firmly believe that Allāh is the Supreme Deity. They used to affirm that Allāh is the Creator of the heavens and earth, and that He, and only He, is All-Powerful. They admitted that their sustenance comes from Allāh, and not from the idols that they used to worship, and they admitted that it was Allāh who would resurrect them after they died. The proof for all this is found in many verses in the Qur'ān.

In the verse quoted by the author, Allāh states that the *Jāhilīyyah* Arabs, if asked who provides their sustenance, or grants them the senses of hearing and sight, or creates life and gives death, or has control over the entire creation, would answer, "Allāh". Yet, despite this belief, they did not have the fear of Allāh, and committed *shirk* with Him.

In another verse, Allāh says,

وَمَا يُؤْمِنُ أَكْثَرُهُم بِٱللَّهِ إِلَّا وَهُم مُّشْرِكُونَ ﴿١٠٦﴾

And most of them do not believe in Allāh except that they commit *shirk* with Him (along with this belief).[37]

In other words, they believe in Allāh, but do not single Him out in worship. So they affirm that Allāh is the Lord, but do not unify Allāh in their worship. Ibn 'Abbās, commenting on this verse, stated, "Their belief in Allāh is that, if you were to ask them who created the skies, and the earth, and the mountains, they would respond, 'Allāh.' Yet, they commit *shirk* (by worshipping others besides Him)."[38] 'Ikrimah, one of the students of Ibn 'Abbās, said, "If you were to ask them who created them, and who created the heavens and earth, they would say, 'Allāh.' So that is the belief that they have of Allāh, but despite this belief, they worship others."[39]

---

[37] Sūrah *Yūsuf*, verse 106.

[38] *Tafsīr al-Ṭabarī,* 16/286.

[39] *Ibid.* 16/286.

Another proof that they believed that Allāh is the Supreme Lord is that the *Jāhilīyyah* Arabs would worship their idols in order to come closer to Allāh (this point will be elaborated on in the third principle). So the fact that the ultimate object of worship was Allāh clearly shows that they considered Allāh to be the Supreme Deity. Yet another proof is that they would call out directly to Allāh in times of distress (this point will be elaborated on in the last principle). Once again, this act shows that the *Jāhilīyyah* Arabs were fully aware that Allāh is the only Deity that is All-Powerful, and that He Alone is the Creator and the Sustainer of all.

So the question arises: if they affirmed all of this for Allāh, then why did they not accept Islām? And why did the Prophet (ﷺ) not consider all of these matters to be sufficient in judging them to be Muslims? For these same people rejected the call of the Prophet (ﷺ), and fought against him, and tried to kill him! And the Prophet (ﷺ) fought them, and considered them to be amongst the worst of mankind.

The answer to these questions lies in knowing the fact that they used to commit *shirk* by worshipping idols along with Allāh. So although they affirmed (in a general sense) the perfect Nature of Allāh (*Tawḥīd al-ʿItiqādī*), they denied that only Allāh deserves to be worshipped, and thus used to direct their acts of worship to other than Allāh, thus rejecting *Tawḥīd al-ʿAmalī*.

And that is why, when the Prophet (ﷺ) came with his simple message of *Lā ilāha illa Allāh*, or, 'There is no deity worthy of worship except Allāh,' they were arrogant, and denied this.

إِنَّهُمْ كَانُوٓا۟ إِذَا قِيلَ لَهُمْ لَآ إِلَٰهَ إِلَّا ٱللَّهُ يَسْتَكْبِرُونَ ﴿٣٥﴾

And when it was said to them, '*Lā ilāha illa Allāh*' they would become arrogant.[40]

And Allāh states that they said, mocking the Prophet's (ﷺ) call,

أَجَعَلَ ٱلْءَالِهَةَ إِلَٰهًا وَٰحِدًا ۖ إِنَّ هَٰذَا لَشَىْءٌ عُجَابٌ ﴿٥﴾

'Has he (Muḥammad) made the objects of worship (into) only one object? Verily this is a very strange matter!'[41]

The Arabs of *Jāhilīyyah* did not reject the Prophet's (ﷺ) message because he called them to believe in the existence of Allāh, or even that Allāh is the Lord and Creator; they already believed this anyway! Rather, they rejected the Prophet's (ﷺ) message because he commanded them to direct all acts of worship to Allāh alone.

---

[40] Sūrah *al-Ṣāffāt*, verse 35.

[41] Sūrah *Ṣād*, verse 5.

Therefore, if one understands that the reason these Arabs of *Jāhilīyyah* were considered outside the fold of Islām, even though they acknowledged Allāh as their Lord, was that they directed acts of worship to other than Allāh, then he will be able to see clearly that it is not sufficient to merely believe that Allāh is the Supreme Lord and Creator in order for one to be considered a Muslim. There is another equally important factor that he must implement, and that is that he must direct all of his acts of worship to Allāh. If he does not do so, then he has fallen into the sin of *shirk*, and resembled the *Jāhilīyyah* Arabs of old, even though he might claim he is a Muslim, and fast and pray and do *Ḥajj* with the Muslims!

To summarise the first principle, we state: it is not sufficient for a person to affirm Allāh's Existence and His Perfect Nature for him to be considered a Muslim. Rather, this affirmation must be followed up by singling out Allāh in worship. If a person does not do so, then he has fallen into the exact same type of *shirk* that the pagan Arabs at the time of the Prophet (ﷺ) fell into, and it is irrelevant whether he calls himself a Muslim or not.

TEXT

The Second Principle

القَاعِدَةُ الثّانِيَة

أنَّهُم يَقُولُونَ : مَا دَعَونَاهُم وَتَوَجَّهْنَا إلَيهِم إلاّ لِطَلَبِ الْقُربَةِ وَالشَّفَاعَة،

فَدَلِيلُ القُرْبَةِ قَولُهُ ـــ تَعَالَى ـــ :

﴿ وَالَّذِينَ اتَّخَذُوا مِنْ دُونِهِ أولِيَاءَ مَا نَعْبُدُهُمْ إلاّ لِيُقَرِّبُونَا إلى اللهِ زُلْفَى إنَّ اللهَ يَحْكُمُ بَيْنَهُمْ فِيمَا هُمْ فِيهِ يَخْتَلِفُونَ إنَّ اللهَ لا يَهْدِى مَنْ هُوَ كَاذِبٌ كَفَّار ﴾

سورة الزمر [٣-٣٩]

وَدَلِيلُ الشَّفَاعَةِ قَولُهُ ـــ تعالى ـــ :

﴿ وَيَعْبُدُونَ مِنْ دُونِ اللهِ مَا لا يَضُرُّهُمْ وَلا يَنْفَعُهُمْ وَيَقُولُونَ هَؤُلاءِ شُفَعَاؤُنَا عِنْدَ اللهِ ﴾، سورة يونس [١٨-١٠]

وَالشَّفَاعَةُ شَفَاعَتَان : شَفَاعَةٌ مَنْفِيَّة وَشَفَاعَةٌ مُثْبَتَة:

فَالشَّفَاعَةُ المَنْفِيَّةُ مَا كَانَتْ تُطْلَبُ مِنْ غَيْرِ اللهِ فِيمَا لا يَقْدِرُ عَلَيْهِ إلاّ الله، وَالدَّلِيلُ قَولُهُ ـــ تَعَالَى ـــ :

﴿ يَا أَيُّهَا الَّذِينَ آمَنُوا أَنْفِقُوا مِمَّا رَزَقْنَاكُم مِنْ قَبْلِ أَن يَأْتِيَ يَوْمٌ لا بَيْعٌ فِيهِ وَلا خُلَّةٌ وَلا شَفَاعَةٌ وَالْكَافِرُونَ هُمُ الظَّالِمُون ﴾ سورة البقرة [٢٥٤-٢]

وَالشَّفَاعَةُ المُثْبَتَةُ هِيَ : الَّتِي تُطْلَبُ مِنَ اللهِ، وَالشَّافِعُ مُكَرَّمٌ بِالشَّفَاعَةِ، وَالمَشْفُوعُ لَهُ : مَنْ رَضِيَ اللهُ قَوْلَهُ وَعَمَلَهُ بَعْدَ الإِذْنِ كَمَا قَالَ ــ تَعَالَى ــ :

﴿ مَنْ ذَا الَّذِي يَشْفَعُ عِنْدَهُ إِلاَّ بِإِذْنِه ﴾ سورة البقرة [٢٥٥-٢]

They (the *mushrikīn*) say,

"We do not supplicate to them and turn toward them except to seek nearness and intercession (with Allāh)."

And the proof of the 'nearness' is in His, the Exalted's saying:

"And those who take protectors besides Him [say], 'We only worship them that they may bring us nearer to Allāh in position.' Indeed Allāh will judge between them concerning that over which they differ. Indeed, Allāh does not guide he who is a liar and [confirmed] disbeliever." [Sūrah *al-Zumar*, verse 3]

And the proof of the 'intercession' is in His, the Exalted's saying:

"And they worship other than Allāh that which neither harms them nor benefits them, and they say, 'These are our intercessors with Allāh.'" [Sūrah *Yūnus*, verse 18]

And there are two types of intercession: *shafā'ah al-manfiyya* (denied and negated intercession); and *shafā'ah al-muthbata* (affirmed and allowed intercession).

As for *shafā'ah al-manfiyya*, it is what is asked from other than Allāh in which there is no power except that of Allāh's. And the evidence for this is in His, the Exalted's saying:

"O you who believe! Spend from that which We have provided for you, before there comes a Day in which there is no exchange [i.e., ransom], and no friendship, and no intercession. And the disbelievers are the wrongdoers." [Sūrah *al-Baqarah*, verse 254]

And *shafā'ah al-muthbata* is that which is asked from Allāh. The one performing the intercession is honoured (by Allāh) due to the intercession. And the one being interceded for is one with whose sayings and actions Allāh is pleased. (The *shafā'ah al-muthbata* occurs) after permission (from Allāh is given), as the Most Exalted said:

"Who is there that can intercede with Him, except by His permission?" [Sūrah *al-Baqarah*, verse 255].

EXPLANATION

This principle deals with two topics. The first topic is the justifications that the *Jāhilīyyah* Arabs used to try to rationalise their *shirk*. And the second topic, which is a follow-up from the first one, and which the author brings up in order to clarify the correct understanding of the topic, is the topic of intercession, or *shafāʿah*. So we will discuss both of these topics in their respective orders.

The Qur'ān mentions the perverted logic that led the *Jāhilīyyah* Arabs to commit *shirk*. They did not believe that their idols were all-powerful, and could grant them what they desired. Nor did they believe that their idols created the world, and provided them with sustenance. Rather, they used these idols as intermediaries in order to approach Allāh. They felt that Allāh was too holy for them to approach directly, thus, they would go through these objects in an attempt to get closer to Allāh. They reasoned that these objects of worship were holy and blessed, and had a high status in front of Allāh, whereas they themselves were sinful, rejected beings who would not be responded to if they called upon Allāh directly. Just like one does not approach a mighty king directly, but rather goes through someone that knows him, so too they would not approach Allāh directly, and go through these idols to approach Him.

So they would say, 'We are only worshipping these idols so that they will raise our requests to Allāh, and bring us closer to Him.' And they would also say, 'We only worship these idols so that they can intercede on our behalf in front of Allāh that our *duʿā* and acts of worship be accepted by Him.' Both of these excuses show that the *Jāhilīyyah* Arabs actually believed that they were approaching Allāh, and thus made Allāh their supreme goal. However, this belief of theirs did not change the fact that they were committing *shirk* by this act. This is because the essence of *tawḥīd* revolves around a *direct* relationship between Allāh and man. Allāh is not in need of any intermediaries in order to accept an act of worship, for Allāh is the All-Powerful, the Knower of all, the Ever-Merciful. By setting up these intermediaries, the *Jāhilīyyah* Arabs were diverting their acts of worship to other than Allāh, even though their ultimate goal was the Pleasure of Allāh!

The example of the 'mighty king' that they use is not applicable to Allāh. This is because any king that is approached is not all-knowledgeable of the situation of his people, so he needs someone to inform him of that situation. Also, in most cases, it is not possible for an average person to approach a king or ruler directly, so he must go through others that know him. Lastly, it is very likely that a ruler or king will not give something to a total stranger or a peasant, but if someone with power and status were to ask him on behalf of this peasant, then he would readily grant him his wish. This is because the king has nothing to gain by giving a lowly peasant his wish, whereas he has a lot to gain by granting a noble or powerful person his wish. And of course all of these matters do not apply to Allāh in the least. He is All-knowledgeable of our situations, and does not need others to inform Him of our needs. And He can be approached by every single created being, for He is nearer to us in His knowledge than our jugular veins. And Allāh is the Ever-Just, and grants to all whom He pleases. He gains nothing from any one of us, but rather we gain everything from Him. Thus, this analogy that they use simply does not apply to Allāh. More importantly, our religion and worship is not based on analogies between Allāh and the creation, but rather on the texts of the Qur'ān and sunnah.

When one understands what has preceded, he will see that the same ruling of *shirk* applies to Muslims in our times who approach the grave of a pious saint, or call out to the dead, believing that these people will act as intercessors between them and Allāh. If a person truly recognises the *shirk* of the *Jāhilīyyah* Arabs, he will see that there is absolutely no difference between the acts that are performed by these Muslim when they call out to their saints, and the *shirk* of the *Jāhilīyyah* Arabs. Both of these people affirm Allāh's Existence, and His All-Powerful Nature. Both of them direct acts of worship to others besides Allāh. And both of them use the exact same excuse when they do these acts – that they are merely trying to come closer to Allāh by going through these 'holy' intermediaries. Yet, this logic is the essence of *shirk*, concerning which the texts of the Qur'ān are very clear.

The *Jāhilīyyah* Arabs Understood the Concept of *ʿIbādah*

Another point of benefit from the verses quoted by the author is that the *Jāhilīyyah* Arabs were fully aware that what they were doing was called 'worship,' because they stated, '...we only worship them that they may bring us nearer to Allāh in position.' So they realised, due to their knowledge of the Arabic language, that what they were doing, of sacrifice, and *duʿā*, and prostration, all counted as *ʿibādah* of these idols. This is in direct contrast to some Muslims of today who commit the same type of *shirk* by approaching Allāh through saints and 'holy' people. However, if you were to ask them why they worship these saints, they would respond, "We do not worship them. We are merely seeking a means to come closer to Allāh, by their intercession, or their blessings, or their status with Allāh."

So these Muslims deny that their actions fall under worship, thus trying to escape from the charge of *shirk* that they deserve. However, the ruling on an act or concept is not dependent on what people call it, it is dependent on the reality and essence of it. If someone were to call *ribā* (interest) 'benefit', it would not change the reality of the fact that it is interest. Likewise, if someone were to call alcoholic drinks 'spirits' or 'refreshments' it does not change the fact that these drinks are alcoholic, and thus prohibited in Islām. If one understands this rule, he will see that these acts, of calling out to dieties, and asking for supernatural help, and seeking a means of pleasing them, all fall under the Islāmic concept of *ʿibādah*. It does not matter whether people refer to them as acts of *ʿibādah* or not; the ruling is based on the reality of the matter, and not its name.

The point is that the *Jāhilīyyah* Arabs realised what they were doing, and admitted it. They openly called their acts directed towards their idols acts of worship. So they were more frank and honest in this regard than the ignorant Muslims who try to change the reality of what they are doing by merely attaching a different label to it.

The Concept of Intercession

The author then mentions the concept of *shafāʿah* in some detail, since this concept is misused in order to justify *shirk*. *Shafāʿah* is the intercession that Allāh allows certain servants of His to perform. The *shafāʿah* is a means that these chosen servants are blessed with to allow people to be saved from the fire of Hell.

There are two types of *shafāʿah* that are mentioned in the Qur'ān.[42] The first type is the *shafāʿah* that is denied or negated, and not accepted by Allāh. This is referred to in many verses, including the one quoted by the author, in which Allāh describes the Day of Judgement as a day in which there will be no *shafāʿah*, meaning that there will be no *shafāʿah manfiyyah* (the negated *shafāʿah*). This type of *shafāʿah* is an intercession that is requested from other than Allāh, or by someone whom Allāh has not granted permission to give *shafāʿah*. So if *shafāʿah* is asked from a false deity, it will never be accepted, because all types of *shafāʿah* are only for Allāh. And if *shafāʿah* is asked by someone who was not granted permission by Allāh to grant *shafāʿah*, this too will not be accepted. This is because *shafāʿah* is a blessing that is granted by Allāh to servants that He chooses. It is *not* a right that certain people can claim from Allāh. No one

[42] The discussion here is regarding the religious concept of *shafāʿah*, which is one in which a person seeks intercession in front of Allāh on behalf of another person that he is forgiven. As for the worldly concept of *shafāʿah*, which is when a person intercedes on behalf of another person for some worldly benefit or gain, this is allowed with two conditions. Firstly, that the desired goal is permissible in and of itself. Secondly, that this intercession does not unjustly take away a right that is due to a specific individual. Allāh states in the Qur'ān, regarding this worldly type of *shafāʿah*: "And whoever intercedes a good (and pure) intercession, then he will share in a part (of the reward)." [Sūrah *al-Nisā'*; 85]

can intercede with Allāh except with Allāh's permission. Therefore, the whole concept of asking various 'saints' to intercede on one's behalf is baseless, for the simple reason that one does not know who will be given permission to intercede on the Day of Judgement.

The second type of *shafā'ah* that is mentioned is the *shafā'ah* that is affirmed and allowed by Allāh. This *shafā'ah* has two conditions to it, as the author alludes to. The first condition has preceded, and is that the person performing the *shafā'ah* be allowed by Allāh to intercede. The second condition is that the one on whose behalf intercession is sought must be one whom Allāh is pleased with. And Allāh is only pleased with those who do not commit *shirk*.

One might ask: what is the point of intercession, when Allāh will decide who intercedes, and He must be pleased with the one on whose behalf intercession is sought? The response is that this fact shows Allāh's Supreme Power and Control over His creation. It is not befitting that a created object have the *right* to intercede in front of Allāh, or to intercede on behalf of anyone. Such a right – if it existed – would go against Allāh's authority and complete Power. Rather, *shafā'ah* is a means of honouring some people, by allowing them to intercede on behalf of others, and it is a means of showing mercy to others, by allowing some people to intercede on their behalf.

These two conditions are mentioned in a number of verses in the Qur'ān. One verse which combines both of these conditions is:

وَكَم مِّن مَّلَكٍ فِي ٱلسَّمَٰوَٰتِ لَا تُغْنِي
شَفَٰعَتُهُمْ شَيْـًٔا إِلَّا مِنۢ بَعْدِ أَن يَأْذَنَ ٱللَّهُ لِمَن يَشَآءُ وَيَرْضَىٰٓ ﴿٢٦﴾

> And there are many angels in the Heavens, whose intercession will be of no use whatsoever, except after Allāh grants permission to whomever He wills, and is pleased.[43]

So even the obedient, sinless angels in the Heavens cannot intercede except after Allāh grants them permission to intercede, and even after this, their intercession will not be accepted, unless Allāh is pleased with the people on whose behalf intercession is sought.

Therefore, when one understands that the *shafā'ah* is totally dependent on Allāh, he sees the futility of asking someone else to intercede on his behalf in front of Allāh.

Without a doubt, the Prophet (ﷺ) has the greatest honour on the Day of Judgement with regards to *shafā'ah*. He will intercede on behalf of his entire nation on the Day of Judgement. But even this intercession is asked *from Allāh*,

---

[43] Sūrah *al-Najm*, verse 26.

and not from the Prophet (ﷺ) himself! It is because of this that, after the call to prayer (*adhān*), the Muslim makes a *du'ā* to Allāh, "O Allāh! The Lord of this Perfect Call, and the Established Prayer! Grant Muḥammad the *Waṣīlah* and Distinction (i.e., the Highest Rank in Paradise) And raise him to the Praised Station (*al-Maqām al-Maḥmūd*, which is the permission to intercede for his nation) that You have promised him, for verily You do not break your promise."[44]

So this *du'ā* is asked *to Allāh*, and not *to the Prophet (ﷺ)*! Likewise, the Companions, who were the most knowledgeable of this nation, never asked the Prophet (ﷺ) after his death to intercede for them, since they knew that after the Prophet's (ﷺ) death, it is not possible to request the Prophet (ﷺ) to do anything. If this is the case with the Prophet (ﷺ), then what is the status of any pious saint in comparison to his (ﷺ) status?

The Prophet (ﷺ) himself pointed out the best way that a person can strive to ensure that he be granted his *shafā'ah* on the Day of Judgement. Abū Ḥurayrah asked him, "O Messenger of Allāh, who will have the greatest chance to gain your intercession on the Day of Judgement?" The Prophet (ﷺ) replied,

> "The one who will have the greatest chance to be granted my *shafā'ah* is he who says: '*Lā ilāha illa Allāh*', sincerely from his heart."[45]

In this ḥadīth, the Prophet (ﷺ) outlined, in clear and explicit terms, that the best way to gain his *shafā'ah* is by practising *tawḥīd*, which entails leaving *shirk* in all its forms. For the one who states this *kalimah* sincerely from his heart must be practising *tawḥīd* and avoiding *shirk*. The irony of all this is that those who do these acts of *shirk* with pious saints and the Prophet (ﷺ) (by invoking upon them as intercessors) do it with the excuse that they want to gain the *shafā'ah* of the Prophet (ﷺ), and yet this act of theirs automatically disqualifies them from his *shafā'ah* because of their *shirk*. So the best way to gain this *shafā'ah* is by avoiding these same acts that are being performed by these people in the name of *shafā'ah*!

To summarise the second principle: the *Jāhilīyyah* Arabs actually intended to come closer to Allāh through the worship of idols and other objects. Their ultimate goal was the Pleasure of Allāh, but they thought that by approaching Allāh through intermediaries, their prayers and worship would be accepted. So when one understands this, he sees that the Muslims who are calling out to saints and prophets, trying to come closer to Allāh and have their prayers

---

[44] Reported by al-Bukhārī (1/152).

[45] Reported by al-Bukhārī, (1/33).

accepted, are in reality committing the exact same type of *shirk* that the *Jāhilīyyah* Arabs committed.

The Third Principle:

TEXT

القَاعِدَةُ الثَّالِثَة

أنَّ النَّبِيَّ صَلَّى اللهُ عَلَيْهِ وَسَلَّمَ ظَهَرَ عَلَى أنَاسٍ مُتَفَرِّقِينَ فِي عِبَادَاتِهِمْ مِنْهُمْ مَنْ يَعْبُدُ المَلائِكَة، وَمِنْهُمْ مَنْ يَعْبُدُ الأنْبِيَاءَ وَالصَّالِحِين، وَمِنْهُمْ مَنْ يَعْبُدُ الأشْجَار و الأحْجَار، وَمِنْهُمْ مَنْ يَعْبُدُ الشَّمْسَ وَالْقَمَر. وَقَاتَلَهُمْ رَسُولُ اللهِ صَلَّى اللهُ عَلَيْهِ وَسَلَّمَ وَلَمْ يُفَرِّقْ بَيْنَهُمْ، وَالدَّلِيلُ قَوْلُهُ ـــ تَعَالَى ـــ :

﴿ وَقَاتِلُوهُمْ حَتَّى لاَ تَكُونَ فِتْنَةٌ وَيَكُونَ الدِّيْنُ كُلُّهُ لله ﴾ سورة الأنفال [٨-٣٩]

وَدَلِيلُ الشَّمْسِ وَالقَمَرِ قَوْلُهُ ـــ تَعَالى ـــ :

﴿ وَمِنْ آيَاتِهِ اللَّيْلُ وَالنَّهَارُ وَالشَّمْسُ وَالْقَمَرُ لاَ تَسْجُدُوا لِلشَّمْسِ وَلاَ لِلْقَمَرِ ﴾ سورة فصلت [٤١-٣٧]

وَدَلِيْلُ الملائِكَةِ قَوْلُهُ ـــ تَعَالى ـــ :

﴿ وَلا يَأمُرَكُمْ أن تَتَّخِذُوا الملائِكَةَ وَالنَّبِيِّيْنَ أرْبَابـًا ﴾ الآيَة - سورة آل عمران [٣-٨٠]

وَدَلِيْلُ الأنْبِيَاءِ قَوْلُهُ ـــ تَعَالى ـــ :

﴿ وَإذْ قَالَ اللهُ يٰعِيْسَى ابْنَ مَرْيَمَ أأنْتَ قُلْتَ لِلنَّاسِ اتَّخِذُونِي وَأُمِّي إلٰهَيْنِ مِنْ دُوْنِ اللهِ قَالَ سُبْحَانَكَ مَا يَكُونُ لِي أَنْ أَقُولَ مَا لَيْسَ لِي بِحَقٍّ إنْ كُنْتُ قُلْتُهُ فَقَدْ عَلِمْتَهُ تَعْلَمُ مَا فِي نَفْسِي وَلا أَعْلَمُ مَا فِي نَفْسِكَ إِنَّكَ أَنْتَ عَلاَّمُ الْغُيُوبِ ﴾ سورة المائدة [٥-١١٦]

وَدَلِيْلُ الصَّالِحِيْنَ قَوْلُهُ ـــ تَعَالى ـــ :

﴿ أولئكَ الَّذِيْنَ يَدْعُونَ يَبْتَغُونَ إلى رَبِّهِمُ الْوَسِيْلَةَ أَيُّهُمْ أَقْرَبُ وَيَرْجُونَ رَحْمَتَهُ وَيَخافُونَ عَذَابَه ... ﴾ الآيَة – سورة الإسراء [١٧-٥٧]

وَدَلِيْلُ الأَشْجَار والأحْجار قَولُهُ ــ تَعالى ــ :

﴿ أفَرَأيْتُمُ الَّلاتَ وَالْعُزَّى وَمَنَاةَ الثَّالِثَةَ الأُخْرَى ﴾ سورة النجم [٥٣-١٩-٢٠]

وحَدِيْثُ أبي وَاقِدٍ اللَّيْثِي ــ رَضِيَ اللهُ عَنْهُ ــ قَالَ : خَرَجْنا مَعَ النَّبيِّ صَلَّى اللهُ عَلَيْهِ وَسَلَّمَ إلَى حُنَيْنٍ وَنَحْنُ حُدَثَاءُ عَهْدٍ بِكُفْر، وَلِلْمُشْرِكِيْنَ سِدْرَةٌ يَعْكِفُونَ عِنْدَهَا وَيَنُوطُونَ بِهَا أَسْلِحَتَهُمْ يُقَالُ لَهَا : ذَاتُ أنْوَاط، فَمَرَرْنَا بِسِدْرَةٍ فَقُلْنَا : يَا رَسُولَ اللهِ اجْعَلْ لَنَا ذَاتَ أنْوَاطٍ كَمَا لَهُمْ ذَاتُ أنْوَاط ... الْحَدِيث.

That the Prophet (ﷺ) came to people who had differences in their (objects of) worship: from them were the worshippers of the angels. And from them were the worshippers of the prophets and the pious. And from them were the worshippers of the trees and the stones. And from them were the worshippers of the sun and the moon. But the Messenger of Allāh (ﷺ) fought them all, and did not consider the differences between them.

And the proof of this (that he fought all of them) is in His, the Exalted's, saying:

"And fight them until there is no *fitnah* and [until] the religion [i.e., worship], all of it, is for Allāh." [Sūrah *al-Anfāl*, verse 39]

And the proof of (worshipping) the sun and the moon in His, the Exalted's, saying:

"And from His signs are the night and the day and the sun and the moon. Do not prostrate to the sun or to the moon, but prostrate to Allāh, who created them, if it should be Him that you worship." [Sūrah *Fuṣṣilat*, verse 37]

And the proof of (worshipping) the angels is in His, the Exalted's saying:

"And they (the prophets) did not order you that you take the angels and the prophets as gods." [Sūrah *Āl-'Imrān*, verse 80]

And the proof of (worshipping) the prophets is in His, the Exalted's saying: "And [beware of the Day] when Allāh will say,

"O Jesus, Son of Mary, did you say to the people, 'Take me and my mother as deities besides Allāh?' He will say, 'Exalted are You! It was not for me to say what I have no right (to say). If I had said it, You would have known it. You know what is within me, and I do not know what is within You. Indeed, it is You who is the Knower of the unseen." [Sūrah *al-Mā'idah*, verse 116]

And the proof of (worshipping) the pious is in His, the Exalted's saying:

"Those whom they invoke seek means of access to their Lord, [striving as to] which of them would be nearest, hoping for His Mercy and fearing His punishment." [Sūrah *al-Isrā'*, verse 57]

And the proof of the (worshipping) of the trees and the stones is in His, the Exalted's saying:

"So have you considered al-Lāt and al-'Uzzā? And Manāt, the third – the other one?" [Sūrah *al-Najm*, verses 19-20].

And (another proof is) the ḥadīth of Abī Wāqid al-Laythī (*raḍiyallāhu 'anhu*), in which he said: "We left with the Prophet (ﷺ) to Ḥunayn and at the time we were close to the period of *kufr* (disbelief). And the pagans had a place of worship upon which they hung their weapons. It was called, '*Dhāt Anwāṭ*.' So when we passed by that place of worship, we said: "O Messenger of Allāh, make for us a place of hanging like they have a place of hanging…".

EXPLANATI

The author, in this principle, is pointing out the different categories of people that existed during the time of the Prophet (ﷺ). Some of them used to worship prophets, such as the Christians, who worship 'Īsa ibn Maryam. Some of them would worship angels and pious people, such as the *Jāhilīyyah* Arabs. Some of them would worship celestial bodies, such as the Sabeans.[46] And of course some would worship rocks and stones as idols, and this was the common practice of the *Jāhilīyyah* Arabs.

The proof for all of these matters is clearly mentioned in the verses quoted by the author.

In the first verse, Allāh states to, '…fight them until there is no tribulations (*fitnah*), and the religion is only for Allāh.' The meaning of *fitnah* in this verse is *shirk*, as Ibn 'Abbās stated.[47] So all types of *shirk* must be fought against. No

---

[46] The Sabeans are referred to in the Qur'ān in three places. There is a great deal of difference regarding who exactly they are, but it appears that they are remnants of a previous nation that followed a prophet of Allāh, and had a complete legal system. However, over the passage of time, they split up into various sects and groups, most of them turning to star worship. They still exist in our times (numbering around thirty thousand), and are known as Mandeans.

[47] See *Tafsīr Ibn Kathīr*, (2/321).

distinction is made between those who worship Jesus Christ or those who worship Rama and Krishna. All false deities and objects of worship must be destroyed, and only the religion of Allāh – based on the pure worship of Allāh – can remain. This verse is like an introduction to the verses that follow. It also shows that the true purpose of *jihad* (fighting in the way of Allāh) is so that only Allāh be worshipped and *shirk* eliminated.

In the second verse, Allāh states that the sun and the moon are only some of His many miracles. They are created by Allāh, and thus do not deserve to be worshipped, '...so do not prostrate to the sun, nor to the moon, but rather prostrate to Allāh who created them, if you are truly believers.'

In the third verse, Allāh reminds the people that they have no proof or basis to worship the angels and prophets, for none of the prophets ever commanded the people to take the angels or prophets as gods besides Allāh. So if even this has not been commanded, then the 'saint worship' that is so common today has even less proof to stand on.

In the fourth verse, Allāh informs us that even the prophets who *are* worshipped did not command their people to worship them. Īsa ibn Maryam, the one who is worshipped as a son of God by the Christians, did not command his people to do this *shirk*. These prophets themselves testify and declare that it is Allāh who is the Lord and the One worthy of worship, and on the Day of Judgement they are going to free themselves of the acts of those who claim to follow them.

In the fifth verse, Allāh mentions the state of pious saints (and angels) who are worshipped besides Allāh, and that they themselves are trying to compete to be closer to Allāh, while hoping for His Mercy and fearing His torment. So is it befitting to worship these people when this is their state? When they themselves are worshipping Allāh, and fearing His Punishment, then what right do others have to worship them? This verse also shows that those people who were truly pious did not command their followers to worship them, for had they done so, it would have caused them to be expelled from the fold of Islām.

In the last verse, the three names given are the names of the famous gods which were worshipped by the *Jāhilīyyah* Arabs before the spread of Islām. Some of these gods were actually people who used to do good deeds, such as feeding the poor and sheltering the traveller. After they died, the Arabs built structures over their graves, and deified them, thus falling into *shirk*.

The final ḥadīth that the author quotes is part of a larger ḥadīth. Abū Wāqid al-Laythī narrates an incident that occurred during the battle of Ḥunayn, when the Companions – most of whom were new to Islām – passed by a tree that the pagans used as a good-luck charm. They would hang their weapons on the tree before going to battle, thinking that this would bring them good luck during the battle. So these new Muslims asked the Prophet (ﷺ) to make for them a similar place that they could seek blessings from as well. When the Prophet (ﷺ) heard this, he exclaimed,

> "Allāh is exalted over what you say! Verily, by Him in Whose Hands is my soul, you have said exactly like the People of Israel before you said, when they said to Moses, 'Make for us a god, just like they have a god.'"

The Prophet (ﷺ) equated their asking for a place of blessing to the asking of the Children of Israel a god to worship. This is because only Allāh blesses certain places and times over others, so by seeking blessings through objects that Allāh has not commanded us to seek blessings through, a person might actually fall into *shirk*.

To summarise this third principle, and the point of all of these verses and ḥadīth: it is irrelevant what is worshipped besides Allāh, for all of it counts as *shirk*. A person can direct an act of worship to a rock or stone, and it will be considered *shirk*. Likewise, he can direct it to the Angel Jibrīl, or the Prophet Muḥammad (ﷺ), or any other prophet, and it will be *shirk*. Just like worshipping the sun and the moon is *shirk*, so too is worshipping a pious saint or a dead person. It is not who is worshipped that defines *shirk*, it is the fact that the object of worship is other than Allāh.

When a person understands this, he realises the futility of those who try to justify *shirk* with the excuse that the *Jāhilīyyah* Arabs worshipped false idols, whereas they go through pious saints and prophets. This can be refuted by two simple points. Firstly, the *Jāhilīyyah* Arabs were of different types. Some of them worshipped idols, and some of them worshipped angels, saints and prophets. But all of them were considered to be pagans outside the fold of Islām. Secondly, *shirk* is not related to the status of the one that is worshipped; it is related to the fact that some deity other than Allāh is worshipped. So even if a person were to worship the most noble of all angels – the Angel Jibrīl, or the best of all of mankind – the Prophet (ﷺ), this would still be considered *shirk*, and this act of his would nullify his *tawḥīd*.

The Fourth Principle — القَاعِدَةُ الرَّابِعَة

TEXT

أنَّ مُشْرِكِي زَمَانِنَا أغْلَظُ شِركـًا مِنَ الأوَّلِيْن، لأنَّ الأوَّلِيْنَ يُشْرِكُونَ فِي الرَّخَاءِ وَيُخْلِصُونَ فِي الشِّدَّة، وَمُشْرِكُوا زَمَانِنَا شِرْكُهُمْ دَائِمٌ؛ فِي الرَّخَاءِ

وَالشِّدَّة . وَالدَّلِيلُ قَولُهُ ـــ تَعالى ـــ :

﴿ فَإِذَا رَكِبُوا فِي الْفُلْكِ دَعَوُا اللهَ مُخْلِصِينَ لَهُ الدِّينَ فَلَمَّا نَجَّاهُمْ إِلى الْبَرِّ إِذَا هُمْ يُشْرِكُونَ ﴾ سورة العنكبوت [٢٩-٦٥]

That the *mushriks* of our time are more severe in *shirk* than those of before, because those of the past committed *shirk* in (times of) ease, but were sincere (to Allāh) in (times of) hardship. However, the *mushriks* of our time are always committing *shirk*, in ease and in hardship. The evidence for this is in His, the Most Exalted's saying:

"And when they board a ship, they supplicate to Allāh, sincere to Him in religion [i.e. faith and hope]. But when He delivers them to the land, at once they associate others with Him." [Sūrah *al-'Ankabūt*, verse 65]

EXPLANATION Although *shirk* is the worst sin that a person can do, it is of various types and levels. So in comparison to other sins, the sin of *shirk* is worse than all of them, but certain acts of *shirk* might be worse than others. For example, it is pure *shirk* to call upon the angels, and it is pure *shirk* to call upon *Shayṭān* as well. Both of these acts are sins that Allāh will not forgive. However, there is no doubt that worshipping the *Shayṭān* is more despicable than other types of *shirk*.

The *mushrikūn* at the time of the Prophet (ﷺ) committed *shirk*. However, at times of distress, they used to turn to Allāh directly, without any intermediaries. This is because they realised that only Allāh could answer their prayers. So when they were in great danger – such as on a boat in a severe tempest – they would turn directly to Allāh, and leave all others besides Him. However, at times of ease and comfort, they would go through their idols and intermediaries to reach Allāh.

Perhaps the story of 'Ikrimah ibn Abī Jahl best demonstrates this point. 'Ikrimah, like his father, was one of the most severe people in his enmity towards the Prophet (ﷺ). Therefore, when the Prophet (ﷺ) entered Makkah as the victor during the Conquest of Makkah, he issued a general amnesty to all its inhabitants, except for four people, one of whom was 'Ikrimah. 'Ikrimah, knowing that he would not be spared due to the harm that he had caused the Muslims, had already fled. He ran away to the sea, and took a boat, hoping to live in a foreign land safely. However, a great storm overtook them while they were at sea, and the people of the boat thought that they would all drown. So they told one another, "Make *du'ā* sincerely to Allāh, for verily all your idols and other gods will be of no help to you now!"

On hearing this, 'Ikrimah said to himself, "By Allāh! If only Allāh can save us in the ocean when we pray sincerely to Him, then He is the only One that can save us when we are on land as well! O Allāh! You have a promise that I make with you, that if you save me from this storm, then I will of a surety go to Muḥammad, and put my hand in his hand, and of a surety I will only find him to be forgiving and generous."

The ship was saved from drowning, and ʿIkrimah fulfilled his promise and went to the Prophet (ﷺ), and indeed, he found the Prophet (ﷺ) to be as he expected, for the Prophet (ﷺ) forgave him, and treated him with respect. And ʿIkrimah proved to be a brave and courageous Muslim, and died as a martyr in one of the battles.[48]

This incident demonstrated to ʿIkrimah the foolishness of his enmity to the call of the Prophet (ﷺ), for the call of the Prophet (ﷺ) was *tawḥīd*. When the people of the boat – who were all idol worshippers – told each other that only Allāh could save them, and their idols were of no use to them, this made ʿIkrimah realise that the implication of this statement was that only Allāh deserved to be worshipped. If only Allāh had the power and capabilities to respond to the call of the one in distress, then what was the point of calling out to these idols and intermediaries?

Therefore the people during the time of the Prophet (ﷺ) realised this simple fact, and only committed *shirk* at times of ease. When they really needed a response, they would call out to Allāh directly. However, those that commit *shirk* in our times are worse than this, because they never call out directly to Allāh. In fact, when they are in a severe situation, they call out to the pious servants and angels of Allāh, and when they are in ease and comfort, they also call out to these same people. So it is common to hear them say, 'O *Ghawth al-Aʿẓam*![49] Help me, Help me!' And another one says, 'O ʿAli! Save me!' And yet another cries out, 'O Messenger of Allāh! Bless me with my need!' So even at times of distress, such Muslims call out to others besides Allāh, proving that the *mushrikūn* of the Prophet's (ﷺ) time were more knowledgeable than these Muslims of today, because the *mushrikūn* were fully aware that only Allāh can respond to their prayers. This is in contrast to these Muslims of today who believe that Allāh is too Exalted for them to approach directly, and thus obligate upon themselves intermediaries to call out to Him.

To summarise the fourth principle: the *Jāhilīyyah* Arabs were more intelligent than the Muslims of our times that commit *shirk*. This is because they realised that only Allāh can respond to their *duʿās*, and therefore would call out to Him

---

[48] See: *al-Iṣābah*, (4/443).

[49] Meaning the "Greatest One in Whom Protection is Sought." This title is appropriate to be applied to Allah, yet the reference is actually to ʿAbd al-Qādir al-Jilani, a pious worshipper of Allāh whose followers in our times deify him with such worship.

sincerely during their times of need. However, the Muslims of our times who commit *shirk* are ignorant of this fact, and call out to their saints at *all* times, thus falling into a worse type of *shirk* than the *shirk* of the *Jāhilīyyah* Arabs.

Calling a Muslim a Disbeliever

Throughout this short treatise, the fact that one who commits *shirk* is a *kāfir* who is outside the fold of Islām was mentioned more than once. However, at the same time, the reader should keep in mind that, once a person states he is a Muslim, and professes to believe in *Lā ilāha illa Allāh Muḥammad Rasūl Allāh*, it is not allowed to label him a disbeliever unless and until he comes forth with an act that clearly and undoubtedly expels him from the fold of Islām. Also, it is essential that the person who does such an act be aware and conscious of the severity of what he is doing, and that he realise that this act is one that takes him out of Islām. In other words, the evidences must be made clear to him, and the proof be established upon him, before he be labelled a *kāfir*.

So it is imperative that one differentiates between an act of disbelief, and a person who is a disbeliever. It is possible that a person does an act of disbelief, and yet not be a disbeliever. For example, if one were to see a Muslim prostrating in front of a grave, then without a doubt this act is one of disbelief. However, it is possible that this particular Muslim did not know that he was prostrating in front of a grave, and was merely offering his *ṣalāt* in that location, ignorant of the fact that there was a grave in front of him. Similarly, it is possible that he is an ignorant Muslim who was merely offering his *ṣalāt* to Allāh at that location, not knowing that it is prohibited to offer his *ṣalāt* in front of a grave. If someone were to label him a disbeliever, merely by seeing him do such an act, and without confirming whether the person realised and understood the severity of what he was doing, he would be mistaken.

Therefore, without a doubt it is the essence of *shirk* to call out to other than Allāh, and prostrate to other than Allāh, and seek supernatural help from other than Allāh. These acts are all acts of disbelief, and, in general, those who perform them are not Muslims. However, the act of labelling a particular individual or group of individuals as disbelievers should not be done by laymen. Rather, such categorisation should only be undertaken by scholars and students of knowledge, for they are the ones who are qualified to make such a definitive ruling.

So the average layman can state that *shirk* includes making *duʿā* to other than Allāh, but when he sees a particular person doing such an act, he should not immediately label him to be a *kāfir*. Rather, he should explain to him that this act is an act of *shirk* and *kufr*, and warn him of the consequences of such an act. As for passing a judgement on a particular individual who claims that he is a Muslim, then he should refrain from doing so, and leave it to those who are qualified.

Conclusion

It is not sufficient that a person professes that Allāh is his only Lord and Creator for him to be a Muslim. Rather, he must follow up this profession with the sincerity of worshipping Allāh alone. This sincerity is essential to one's Islām, and to fall short of it nullifies his claim to be a Muslim. For the essence of Islām – in fact, the very purpose of creation – is so that Allāh alone is worshipped, and all other false deities are opposed. And it does not matter whether this 'deity' is an evil person, or a false idol, or the most pious of mankind, for all such acts are acts of *shirk* that Allāh has promised He will never forgive. Likewise, it is irrelevant whether one believes that these false deities are themselves all-powerful and can respond to their request, or they merely use them to approach Allāh and seek a means of nearness to Him. Both of these instances are clear cases of *shirk*.

TEXT

والله أعلم

وَصَلَّى اللهُ عَلَى مُحَمَّدٍ وَآلِهِ وَصَحْبِهِ وَسَلَّم .

And Allāh knows best, and may the extolation and peace of Allāh be upon Muḥammad, and his family and companions.

EXPLANATION

The author concludes his short treatise by the phrase, 'Allāh knows best,' implying that this is the limit of his knowledge, and that perfection is only with Allāh. This is indicative of his modesty and humbleness.

He then prays that Allāh send His *salām* upon the Prophet (ﷺ), and his family and companions. And the *salām* of Allāh upon His prophet is that He mentions Him in the Highest Company of angels. And the *salām* of the believers upon him is that they pray to Allāh to bless him, and raise his status in Paradise, and reward him the best of all rewards. For indeed, the Prophet (ﷺ) is our role model, and what a noble role model he is!